Last of the 39'ers

Sean Feast

Last of the 39'ers

The Extraordinary Wartime Experiences of Squadron Leader Alfie Fripp

Sean Feast

Grub Street · London

Published by
Grub Street
4 Rainham Close
London
SW11 6SS

A CIP record for this title is available from the British Library

ISBN-13: 9781909166158

Cover design by Sarah Driver
Design by Sarah Driver
Edited by Sophie Campbell

Printed and bound by Berforts Group, UK

Grub Street Publishing only uses
FSC (Forest Stewardship Council) paper for its books.

Contents

FOREWORD

In 2009 a group of ex-prisoners of war visited the site of Stalag Luft III at Sagan in Poland for the sixty-fifth anniversary of the Great Escape. The press came too and quickly identified a character, the impish Alfie. Not only was Alfie a character but he was also a '39-er', shot down and captured on October 16, 1939. So Alfie became the focus for their reporting of our visit. Television became interested in his story, and Alfie made further visits to Sagan, one in the company of Sir David Jason. He was a natural for television with his looks and sly humour. He thrived on it.

But Alfie had a serious side too as is manifest in this book. His death in January, when the book was only part written, was a setback for its author but Sean Feast had drawn from Alfie and his family and friends enough material to complete his splendid story, a work that catches Alfie's lively spirit and reflects it throughout the book.

In the prison camps in which we were held, Alfie was a prominent figure. His appearance in the barracks was always welcome because Alfie was in charge of Red Cross food parcels. But, much more than that, he was our Red Cross representative. It was he who sent requests for sporting gear, musical instruments, books and much else, he who maintained a meticulous correspondence with the Red Cross, reporting on health and other aspects of life in the camp. Sean has included some of Alfie's letters. They are impressive, showing a conscientious and thoughtful man who would do anything to improve the lot of his fellow captives.

Alfie also played a part in the camp intelligence. The camp leader, the magnificent

James 'Dixie' Deans, was able to spirit information to MI9 in London; Alfie and Sammy Panton, who was in charge of the post, worked together when mail came in, especially parcels of which they had been notified to look out for and in which information and escape material were hidden. Alfie never had time to be bored: if he wasn't at the railhead collecting parcels, supervising their transport to the camp and in due course personally delivering them to the barracks, or dealing with the Red Cross or sneaking parcels from the sight of German censors, he was rehearsing for an appearance on the Stalag stage.

Alfie was a remarkable man and Sean has been inspired to write, what for me is a memorable book

Calton Younger

—AUTHOR'S INTRODUCTION—

I was introduced to Alfie Fripp through the good auspices of Colin Higgs, a fellow author and enthusiast, in the late summer of 2012. Having seen David Jason's documentary on the Great Escape, I was of course aware of Alfie, but had not until that time had the pleasure of meeting him. Colin told me that Alfie was interested in working with an author to help write his autobiography but had not, until that time, come across anybody he especially got on with!

It was therefore with some trepidation that I drove down to the south coast to meet this gallant airman, conscious of the fact that I could swiftly join the ranks of those who had already been seen and deemed not up to the mark. I need not have worried. Alfie was charm personified and particularly pleased that I not only knew but had previously written about his first Blenheim pilot, Johnnie Greenleaf, who had also been his best man. It was rewarding to be able to tell this distinguished gentleman a little about Johnnie's wartime service, and I was only too pleased to present Alfie with a copy of *The Pathfinder Companion* (Grub Street, 2012) with mentions of his former friend and colleague. I think it was this, perhaps more than anything else, that sealed our partnership and I was eager to get Alfie's story underway.

The usual order of things (at least for me) is to conduct a series of interviews and complement those interviews with concurrent research, going back over what has been said to check the facts, dates, times, personalities etc as accurately as feasible and against first source and contemporary documents (wherever possible). We had completed the third of these interview sessions when Alfie was taken ill with what seemed to be an innocuous ear infection. I was not especially alarmed; we had reached the stage in Alfie's story when he had been shot down and captured, and I was very much looking forward to hearing more of his adventures in the camps that he had already outlined when I received a phone call I had been dreading. Alfie had taken off on his final flight and would not be returning.

This left me in a little bit of a quandary. Alfie's story was always meant to be an autobiography, with me in the background to allow the great man to take the deserving centre stage. But I knew it would be wrong to invent words that had never been spoken, or guess at feelings that had never been expressed. With the full support of his family, and my publisher, I was asked if I would finish Alfie's story, and do so as a biography using as many of Alfie's actual words, thoughts and expressions as possible.

With my first-hand notes, and a selection of Fripp family archive recordings, I was able to bring together the missing components into what I hope is a flowing narrative. Colin Higgs again also came to the rescue by allowing me access to many hours of interviews he had recorded with Alfie only a few months earlier. Friends and family also introduced me to former Kriegies Cal Younger, Andy Wiseman, Charles Clarke and Eric Hookings who were able to give me valuable insight into what life must have been like for Alfie in the camps. So many people were eager to help that it confirmed, if any such confirmation was needed, that Alfie's story had to be finished, so that others might recognise the achievements of a man who came to be known as 'the last of the 39-ers'.

I hope my critics will look favourably on this work and understand the path I was obliged to take, and my reasons for doing so. I hope my reader will agree with me that Alfie's story is a remarkable one, and it is a great pity that he did not live long enough to enjoy its publication, and a few precious moments in the limelight that might have resulted.

Sean Feast
Sarratt, Hertfordshire
October 2013

──────────PROLOGUE──────────

Sergeant Alfie Fripp, a recently-qualified observer with 57 Squadron, had no intention of dying that day, or any other day for that matter. But on the morning of October 16, 1939, he came frighteningly close.

───────────

The war was a little over six weeks old and not a great deal seemed to be happening. The Germans had swept into Poland and scared the Poles and half of Europe with their new Blitzkrieg style of warfare, a lightning war with highly-mobile armour and air support. Alfie's squadron had received orders shortly after the general mobilisation to proceed from its peacetime base at Upper Heyford in Oxfordshire to France via Southampton, the advance party setting off on September 12 and the main body following ten days later.

The train took the ground crews and the squadron's administrative contingent from Bicester, a surprisingly-easy journey through the pleasant Hampshire countryside to the south coast, where they set sail to join a convoy then assembling at Spithead. It was not until the small hours of the morning, however, that the convoy had finally assembled and they did not reach Cherbourg until the early afternoon of the 24th when they disembarked to await another troop train to take them south. Cherbourg was alive with men in uniforms of all different hues, and while there was a sense of anticipation, there was nothing of the chaos and panic that would come later – much later – by which time his war would anyway be over.

Their destination first off was the town of Roye, to the east of Amiens, and thence to the small village of Amy, four miles further south, where Alfie and the others would join them. As aircrew, he did not have to suffer the tedium of a long journey over land and sea, but was able to fly direct to his new home instead.

It didn't seem much like they were going to war, but rather another one of the squadron's annual exercises. Travelling light, save for the obligatory kitbag comprising his white pre-war flying overalls and a few other essentials, Alfie and his Irish pilot, Mike Casey, flew over the channel in two flights of nine aircraft each. Looking down below, the water looked beguiling, at least to someone like Alfie who had been destined for a life on the ocean waves but whose ambitions had been, quite literally as it happens, cut short.

They landed at Amy, a pretty village with a rather impressive church, and while the officers and NCOs (Alfie was by now a sergeant) were given quarters in various houses scattered about the place, humble airmen had to sleep in neighbouring farms, using straw for bedding. There was little in the way of sanitation or washing facilities, but since they were to spend most of their time flying, it did not seem to matter.

The aerodrome was guarded by a contingent of French military, who as well as providing protection, also supplied the men with the rations in the first few days. Alfie spent the next twenty-four hours settling in, and had to wait a further twenty-four hours before the outstanding transport finally arrived, and the squadron began to place itself more onto a war footing. In the meantime, one of the flight commanders and a handful of airmen made for the town of Metz to the east of Verdun and close to the border with Germany, where they were to establish a forward air base. An alternative base was also established at Étain.

The order of the day so early in the war was not one of bombing military targets but rather undertaking what were known as 'strategic reconnaissance' trips, spying out what the Germans were up to and where they might strike next. The Blenheims would first fly to Metz where they would be refuelled, and thence into Germany, usually to the north west, and afterwards to fly back to the UK, Manston or Hendon, depending on the state of their fuel reserves. At least that was the theory. No-one seemed to question what would happen to those fuel reserves if they were being chased by a fighter!

There was a false start on the afternoon of October 10 when two aircraft took off to Metz but returned two days later, bad weather having prevented any further flying. The lack of any real action was beginning to show, aircrew were becoming frustrated and the rather squalid conditions were adding to their woes as Alfie recalls:

"We were, we felt, highly-trained, highly-professional flying men who were at the very top of their game. We also had, in our minds, one of the finest aircraft of the time – the snub-nosed Blenheim I – which the aircraft's manufacturers (Bristol) assured us could pretty much outfly and outrun anything we were ever likely to encounter. It had a claimed top speed of 259 mph at 13,000ft and was the fastest bomber in the world. Unfortunately, it didn't prove fast enough, as we were very soon to find out.

"Only a few weeks before, our former wingco [Wing Commander W L Payne] had been replaced by a new squadron commander, Wing Commander Harry Day. Known on the squadron as 'Pricky' but more widely as 'Wings', Day was a 'type', a regular officer of the public school variety (although virtually every officer at that time was a product of the boarding school system) who at forty was considerably older than the rest of the men under his command, me included. He was at times distant and rather aloof, and had not helped his cause by mixing up the crews. There was good logic for doing so – spreading the experience throughout the squadron – but I had become rather used to my pilot, Johnnie Greenleaf, and partly resented being crewed with Mike.

"Given his age, Day may well have been able to sit out the war in a staff role, but had virtually begged to be given operational command. Whether I liked him or not, he was clearly a man who felt the need to lead from the front, and he was determined to fly the squadron's very first wartime operation."

It happened on the morning of October 13, a Friday of all days, when the wingco and his crew comprising Sergeant Eric Hillier (his observer) and Aircraftman Frederick Moller (his wireless op/air gunner) finally took off from Metz (in Blenheim L1138) to undertake a reconnaissance of roads and railways between Hamm, Hannover and Soest. Exactly an hour later, the chosen pilot from B Flight, Flying Officer Clive Norman, also took off. Norman completed an eventful but wholly unsuccessful sortie, reached England late in the afternoon and crashed. Of the wing commander's aircraft, however, there was no news. The adjutant simply wrote the words 'Did not return' in the squadron's operations record book (ORB) and the three men were posted 'Missing'. It was not an auspicious start, and it would be some time later that Alfie would learn their fate, shot down by a marauding fighter and two of their number killed.

Only three days after their commanding officer's loss, it was Alfie's turn. The briefing provided to Mike Casey from 70 Wing Headquarters, such as it was, was at best 'vague':

"We were a reconnaissance squadron and so we were to undertake reconnaissance of an area in the west of Germany near the Siegfried line and particularly look out for anything suspicious on the Dutch/ Belgium border. Then it was home in time for tea, albeit that we had a choice of where we wanted to take it! One of the areas we were to reconnoitre was Münster, but I do not recall anyone telling us that it was a Luftwaffe fighter headquarters and home to three crack German fighter squadrons with pilots fresh from the blitz against Poland.

"We got changed in what was now a very crowded crew room and I pulled on my white overalls – the squadron badge on the breast pocket suitably removed in case we were shot down. We did not want to make the Germans a present of who we were. Then with our parachutes gathered, and other accoutrements such as my map case and charts, three of us – myself, Flying Officer Mike Casey (my new pilot), and Aircraftman 'Paddy' Nelson our wireless op/air gunner – clambered into our waiting Blenheim (L1141) to undertake the obligatory pre-flight checks."

With the checks completed, and Alfie settled into his navigator's position to the right of his pilot in the front of the nose, Mike started the engines and they began taxiing across the grass field for take-off. The Blenheim had many faults, but few could fault the visibility afforded to the pilot and navigator by the front nose, which was almost entirely perspex. They sat together much as you would in the front seat of a motorcar, which made communication far easier. It also left them feeling somewhat exposed.

"The short trip to Étain was uneventful, and the ground crews refuelled us in double-quick time. At 11.00hrs, we set out for Germany.

"We had been promised a fighter escort. The Air Component and Advanced Air Striking Force then in France had various Hurricane squadrons at their disposal but they must have been busy elsewhere for while we waited, they never showed up. It was with a certain amount of grumbling that we were obliged to proceed to the target on our own.

"Mike took the Blenheim in a steady climb up to about 10,000ft and we stooged around where we thought the target should be. I had little, or nothing, in terms of navigational aids (certainly compared to the systems that later bomber crews would receive) but was fairly confident regarding our position. We were just above the cloud base, and needed to get down below it to gather any meaningful intelligence. Mike therefore pushed the stick forward and we gradually descended until we could visually confirm our target and allow the camera in the bomb well to start turning over and create the perfect line overlap."

Even with the cloud it was a beautiful day but it very soon turned ugly. First Alfie began to see the occasional flak burst – dirty little smudges to spoil an otherwise perfect sky. Every one of those smudges, however, represented a high-velocity shell exploding, sending deathly shards of hot metal across the sky. They did not want to be too near when one of those things burst, and Mike began some simple alterations in course and height so as to keep the gunners guessing:

"We had the choice of whether we made for England or one of our airfields in France, and Mike decided to try for the former, asking me to give him the appropriate course. The flak had now stopped and that could only mean one thing: that we were not alone. Mike began searching for and using what little cloud cover was available, just as Paddy gave a short report on the intercom that he could see an enemy aircraft approaching fast. Mike opened up the throttles to increase speed, and there was a notable surge from the two Mercury engines as he sought to get the maximum speed out of our aircraft. It wasn't enough. The fighter, which Paddy identified as a Messerschmitt Bf109, easily caught us and opened fire while it was still in a climb.

"Mike dived for the deck in a desperate battle to shake the fighter off our tail, performing a series of death-defying stunts at zero feet but without effect. Mike wasn't the best pilot on the squadron but that day he flew like the devil. While the German pilot no doubt marvelled at his adversary's pluck and determination, the outcome was inevitable. At last, after another burst of fire from the enemy fighter, Mike misjudged his height, clipped the top of a tree and we went down."

In some respects Alfie's war was over; in another it was only just beginning.

CHAPTER ONE

——————SHORTCOMINGS——————

It may sound strange that a man so steeped in the traditions of the senior service should ultimately carve out a career for himself in the Royal Air Force. But it had everything to do with his height.

———————————

Alfred George Fripp – 'Bill' to his family and 'Alfie' to everyone else – was born on June 13, 1914 into a military family. His father was a regular in the Royal Marines, an NCO, who was incredibly proud of a service career that had lasted more than two decades. He was often overseas, including tours in Gallipoli and Zeebrugge during the First World War.

Alfie was one of six children – three boys and three girls – and remembers a happy childhood where his father kept discipline simply by raising his voice. As often happens in a military family, however, the real disciplinarian in the house was his mother, and she worked tirelessly to keep the family unit together, working all hours to make ends meet:

> "They were a wonderful couple, living on virtually nothing – about thirty shillings a week. It was hard going: mother was sewing on buttons on Marine shirts to earn a little extra money and to see us through the war."

In the early years Alfie lived at the Royal Marines barracks at Gosport before moving to the barracks at Eastleigh (at one end of Portsmouth island) where his father was promoted company sergeant major. From the outset, both his mother and father were keen that at least one of their children should pursue a career in the military. His mother, an accomplished seamstress, loved uniforms with brass buttons, and so it was a foregone conclusion that some service was beckoning for at least one of their male offspring.

Using his military connections, his father secured a place for Alfie at the Royal Hospital School in Greenwich (now home to the National Maritime Museum) and it was into these hallowed halls that he was marched as a very young and – at the time – very innocent eleven-year old:

> "I left home for the first time and remember crying my eyes out. I was then vaccinated and inoculated and for three weeks suffered from infected scabs.
>
> "Like many such educational establishments in the 1920s, there was nothing easy or soft about the RHS. Indeed by modern standards it might even have been considered brutal. Every day, come winter or summer, we started with a circuit or six around the parade square in just our PT vests and little else before having a shower and then breakfast. Then we would make our way to the lecture rooms where lessons would begin."

A number of the teachers were especially keen to display their more masochistic tendencies; the headmaster, 'Nobby' Lumsden, took particular delight in dishing out the cane for even the smallest misdemeanour including not paying attention in class. Many boys of Alfie's generation received the cane, but the vigour with which Mr Lumsden seemed to exert his authority was a little too enthusiastic for Alfie's liking, to the point that the man appeared to take a running jump!

Lumsden was a civilian, whereas the vast majority of instructors were of course naval men, typically petty officers. These POs were no less brutal, and were often armed with a 'Turks Head' – a small, knotted length of rope with which to beat the boys for even the most innocent and trivial transgression. Arguments between boys were not settled in the comfort of the headmaster's office, or even in a boxing ring, but in a bear-knuckle fight.

Whilst at Greenwich Alfie managed to contract diphtheria, a highly-contagious and – at the time – highly-dangerous disease that affected his breathing:

> "I was sent to the Great Northern Hospital for three weeks enduring enemas every other day and injections every day. Then I had ten weeks convalescence to get me fit again. While I was at home,

Alfie at school in his naval uniform.

recovering over Christmas, I heard that Lord Allington was having a shoot and didn't have any beaters. I asked him how much he was paying and he said it was three shillings a day. I worked for him for five days and gave all but five shillings of my earnings to my mother."

The time spent in hospital put Alfie behind with his studies but he soon caught up. He also kept his nose clean, finding himself in no more or less trouble than any of his contemporaries:

"I must have learned something for I succeeded in passing my exams and securing a place in the upper school (much like a grammar school) where the pace of learning increased dramatically. We were taught a vast array of subjects and disciplines such as seamanship, navigation and astronomy, with lectures on Saturday mornings rather than fatigues, all with the purpose of becoming an artificer apprentice and joining the Royal Navy."

But then Alfie suffered his first major setback, and his mother's dream of seeing him in a smartly-buttoned tunic appeared to evaporate. He was too small. Although he passed his exams, finishing in the first 100 out of 1,700 candidates, he failed the medical. At only 4ft 10ins, he was two inches too short for the required 5ft they were looking for. To the young lad at that time, it was a humiliation little short of a disaster. He had spent the previous three years with a single purpose, and now that purpose had been destroyed. Then fate took a hand:

"Our careers master, an ex chief petty officer, said that if I couldn't join the navy, then the Royal Air Force might have me. The RAF was not so particular about height, and was actively looking for apprentices at its training facility in Halton. Through his good auspices I applied for a place and the test papers were sent through to the school. The exam suited my aptitude: I was fairly good at English, and the questions around navigation suited my learning. It was with delight, though perhaps not surprise, that I was offered a place, and so on September 30, 1930 I found myself with a travel warrant in my pocket arriving at the railway station at Wendover, waiting for transport to take me to RAF Halton for training as a Trenchard 'Brat'.

"Halton is a well-known training establishment with a proud record, and is an important part of our armed forces, even today. The first three days were spent with various medicos pushing and prodding in places I had rather they hadn't, making sure I was fit for purpose. Some boys failed at this point, usually because of their eyesight and were packed off before we even knew their names.

"After that, we were interviewed and divided according to our particular specialism: mine was wireless, and so I found myself posted with sixty-eight others (out of a total 550 aircraft apprentices in the 22nd Entry) to Cranwell for training as electricians and wireless operator mechanics."

Cranwell suited keen, fresh youngsters like Alfie perfectly: if you wanted to be busy, you could be. There was always plenty to do, especially if you liked sport. Indeed there was every manner of sport to play, and quite a few more besides. Alfie was particularly minded towards hockey, as a goalkeeper; he found that he was always in demand. He also enjoyed swimming, very quickly achieving his RAF swimming certificate of which he was immensely proud. The quality of instruction was exceptional, and additional tuition was always available and encouraged.

It was a culture shock compared to what he had been used to. He had moved from a very harsh, very disciplinarian environment at Greenwich to one that was much less brutal and much more inclusive. Of course there was discipline, but it was within the realms of what one would consider 'normal' within a service. The camaraderie was also worthy of note: the friendships formed as an apprentice were friendships for life, and among his contemporaries was Johnnie Greenleaf who would later become Alfie's pilot and best man at his wedding. Johnnie also went on to a thoroughly-eventful career in Pathfinder Force, winning the 'double' of both the distinguished service order (DSO) and the distinguished flying cross (DFC) for bravery in action against the enemy[*].

---

[*]The 22nd Entry included a number of 'Brats' who went on to distinguish themselves in the war that followed. First among them, undoubtedly, was the great Roy Ralston who went on to complete more than ninety bomber operations including twenty-one consecutive attacks against Berlin. A noted low-level expert, his list of decorations included two DSOs, the Air Force Cross (AFC) and the distinguished flying medal (DFM). Another distinguished 'bomber boy' was Alan Cousens, a Pathfinder squadron commander who by the time of his death in 1944 was a wing commander with the DSO, DFC and the Czech Military Cross (MC). Two 'Brats' who went on to become Battle of Britain pilots of note included John Craig who shot down at least five enemy aircraft and probably four more, and was awarded the DFM. The second was Harry Steere who similarly became an 'ace' before moving to Pathfinder Force and winning the DFC and DFM. Both men did not survive the war. Although Alfie did not know any of these men well – since they were not on his course – a 'Brat' was almost always immediately identifiable, and the invisible bond that existed between these men and others both before and after was automatic and unquestioned.

At Cranwell, Alfie was attached to 2 Flight, under the watchful eye of Corporal Nightingale (who Alfie met up with many years later as a squadron leader – the war was kind when it came to promotion!). Nightingale was generally well liked – certainly compared to other NCOs at that time – and was a notable gymnast. Alfie also listened to the advice of the senior boys allocated to each flight who helped him unpack and settle in. They also taught him such practical disciplines as how to lay out his locker and make his bed to avoid the unwanted attention of the NCOs.

The budding airman had leaned towards E&W not just because of a liking of wireless, nor because of any technical aptitude, although both no doubt played some part in his decision-making. It was actually because he wanted to fly. Alfie recognised early on that aircraft would always need a wireless operator.

But for the first six weeks or so, Alfie didn't see much of a wireless for his time was taken up almost entirely with drill and physical training (PT in knee-length dark blue shorts and vests with Cambridge blue bands at the neck and arms), learning how to march, run, jump and climb to his instructors' satisfaction. He was issued with a bayonet and a rifle and told how to clean them, such that they were always in pristine working order.

They were all, about this time, given what they would today call an 'air experience' flight which amounted to little more than ten minutes with an instructor taking the often-terrified pupils on a short circuit or two around the field:

> "We flew in a De Havilland Puss Moth, which at the time was still quite a new aeroplane, with a high wing and three seats. It was considered one of the highest performance private aircraft of that era, and in the hands of our instructor – a former Royal Flying Corps pilot called Cuthbert Bazell – it was quite an experience. Flight Lieutenant Bazell had a crooked neck that was always leaning to port (I think it was as a result of an accident), so he used to take off and land with the starboard wing low to adjust his line of sight!"*
>
> "Cranwell was of course an officer training school, and every Saturday morning, after we had finished our cleaning chores, we would make our way to the airfield to watch the cadets learning to fly. Some of us who were bold enough would see if we could

---

*Flight Lieutenant Cuthbert Caumont Bazell, formerly of the Somerset Light Infantry. Later group captain OBE. He died in January 1975 at the age of eighty-two.

cadge a flight, and so it was that I managed to steal my first flight in an ageing Avro 504 which was a different experience again from the Puss Moth. I marvelled that the aircraft was able to build up sufficient speed to get off the ground."

The E&W syllabus comprised basic electrics and wireless construction, wireless operating, recognition of aircraft electrical systems, and training in petrol sets and power supplies. The students also spent considerable time in the workshop practicing on a four-and-a-half inch Denham lathe making various machine parts. It was expected of them to be able to fashion repairs to their equipment in an emergency, even if that meant making new parts from scratch.

"The course also included instruction in all manner of signalling: morse; semaphore; and Aldis lamp in particular. Morse I found comparatively straightforward; it was all about practice and became automatic over time. There is a rhythm to Morse such that you can recognise an individual's 'style', not unlike a musician's. I passed our exam with a speed of twenty-five words per minute. Semaphore and Aldis were also a question of practice and patience. Our instructors were, ironically, both naval men and used to 'speak' to one another by making semaphore signals with their hands, not unlike a form of sign language. It proved to be a very useful way of communicating in a noisy aeroplane."

Alfie soon became accustomed to the routine of Cranwell life and gave neither his instructors nor the disciplinary NCOs cause for concern. Punishment for misdemeanours was measured in the number of days 'confined to camp' (CC), and during Alfie's time, statistics showed that Cranwell boys achieved a higher percentage rate per head than their Brat colleagues at Halton! The most heinous of crimes was smoking (for those who did not have permission) which for a second offence could result in the offender being confined to camp for fourteen days. CCs were also meted out for such offences as talking in church (seven days), two inches of dust beneath their lockers (also seven days) and the print not buffed off the side of a boot polish tin (three days). Alfie tended to be less bothered by the pettiness of the Cranwell 'rules' and more focused on what to do during the several hours that he was permitted 'off duty':

"There was a disadvantage to being in Cranwell, and that was its location. We were often allowed out of camp; we had to be back in time for roll call at 9.00pm and once a month we had an extended pass until midnight, but there was nowhere to go. Sleaford was the nearest town, but since we were not allowed to keep a car, and the buses were infrequent at best, our social life was almost non-existent. We had to console ourselves by dreaming about the AOC's daughter!"

His three years at Cranwell ended in September 1933, and Alfie passed out as a nineteen-year-old aircraftman, first class (AC1), wireless operator mechanic (WOM), his proficiency being described as 'satisfactory'. Indeed the majority of his contemporaries received the same rating and became AC1s.*

————————

The air officer commanding (AOC), Royal Air Force, Halton, was Air Vice-Marshal N D K MacEwen, CMG, DSO but the Cranwell 'Brats' had their own passing-out parade, a relatively-modest affair conducted by the AOC Cranwell, Air Vice-Marshal Arthur Longmore. They then kept a keen eye on the notice boards as they awaited their first posting.

Shortly before the war, and certainly after war had broken out, aircrew had little choice in where they were posted. There are many stories of potential fighter pilots being posted to bomber squadrons and vice versa, almost as if the air force was playing some cruel game. But in the autumn of 1933, when Alfie qualified, he was asked where he wanted to go and listed his desired postings in the following order:

————————

*From the official report at the time: of the 550 boys originally attested: sixty-nine were posted to the Electrical and Wireless School for training as electricians and wireless operator mechanics; eight were granted discharge by purchase; twenty-one were discharged as 'unlikely to become efficient airmen'; nine were discharged on medical grounds; three were remustered to Aircrafthand; four died; twelve were transferred to junior entries and fourteen were transferred from senior entries, leaving 438 to pass-out from Halton.

As a result of the final examinations: sixty-nine aircraft apprentices, were classified as leading aircraftmen; 323 were classified as aircraftmen, first class; thirty-eight were classified as aircraftmen, second class; three aircraft apprentices failed to qualify; and five were not examined owing to sickness. The report states: 'the number of apprentices of this entry who have been classified as either Leading Aircraftmen or Aircraftmen, First Class, is approximately 90 per cent. This is the highest percentage of any entry on passing-out.'

Upper Heyford; Boscombe Down; Abingdon; and Calshot. The first three foretold a career in bombers, perhaps flying the lumbering Vickers Virginia, Fairey Hendon or Handley Page Heyfords then in service. Calshot offered something vastly different, and potentially more exciting:

> "I knew that at Calshot (where Southampton Water joins the Solent) there was an established flying-boat base, and for a man who wanted to fly, flying boats seemed to present the best opportunity. They were an aircraft that needed a crew, and especially the skills of a wireless operator. To me this was the best of all worlds: not only would I be flying, but I would also be close to the sea!"

Alfie officially moved to Calshot (base) on February 16, 1934, and in the best traditions of the Royal Air Force was immediately instructed by his flight sergeant to sweep the hangar! Six weeks later, on April 1, 1934 (the sixteenth anniversary of the foundation of the RAF), he was formally posted to 201 (Flying Boat) Squadron, the first of the two flying boat squadrons with which Alfie would serve over the next five years.

Not much has been written about flying boats and the flying-boat squadrons of the 1930s, certainly not from an operational standpoint, and there are very few airmen left who experienced both the delight – and the occasional unwelcome excitement – of flying such primitive aeroplanes for hours at a time over stretches of hundreds of miles of often hostile seas.

The 201 Squadron that Alfie was posted to had, of course, originally been part of the Royal Naval Air Services (RNAS). All RNAS units simply added the prefix of '200' to their former squadron number, so as No. 1 Squadron RNAS it became 201 Squadron Royal Air Force. Having been disbanded not long after the end of the First World War, it was reformed at Calshot in 1929, and by the time Alfie arrived on February 16, the squadron was commanded by Squadron Leader Cecil Wigglesworth AFC.

Wigglesworth was quite a character, especially to a humble AC1 like Alfie. He had assumed command in the spring of 1933 from Squadron Leader Edward Turner AFC, and from what they heard about Turner, Wigglesworth was the complete opposite. A veteran of the RNAS and a First World War airship pilot, he was also a talented cricketer (a right-handed bat for those that know about such things). But his most notable claim to fame was that he was believed to have been the inspiration for Biggles, the eponymous hero of W E Johns. Alfie certainly believed it, for Wigglesworth was a man who got things done and of whom many stood in awe. Alfie was mostly in awe of his age, for although he was only forty, he looked like an old man!

Not long after he arrived, and since he was not yet attached to a regular crew, a number of 'one-off jobs' came Alfie's way, one of which he particularly remembers:

> "We received a request for a wireless operator to go as part of a small
> group in a power boat down to Portland, where we would then pick
> up and return a number of fuelling barges needed at Calshot. The
> trip down was a pleasure cruise at a steady twelve knots, and we
> arrived at Portland shortly before nightfall. I didn't have a great deal
> to do, other than send the occasional wireless signal to report our
> progress. The journey home, however, was somewhat more laborious.
> The barges were only capable of four knots at best, so we amused
> ourselves by sending a signal to the battleship, HMS *Nelson*. The
> battleship had embarrassingly run aground, so we asked them if they
> needed a tow! Needless to say their unofficial reply is unprintable."

He had been on the squadron for some weeks before he was finally given his chance
to fly in one of its boats (all aircraft in flying-boat squadrons should technically be
referred to as 'boats'): the magnificent Supermarine Southampton.

Before he arrived at Calshot, Alfie had never seen a Southampton up close, and
compared to the Avro 504 and Puss Moth, it was enormous. The length of the
aircraft (51ft) and its wingspan (75ft) could have made her look somewhat clumsy,
but Alfie thought her a beautiful beast, and powerful with it. Its two 502 hp Napier
Lion V engines gave her a top speed of only fractionally more than 100 mph at sea
level, and a cruising speed of just over 80 mph. But with a maximum range of more
than 900 miles, the purpose for which she was intended was clear.

The Southampton had achieved fame for a series of long-distance flights that
later helped persuade the powers-that-be of the possibilities of establishing a base
in Singapore. She was also famed for her reliability, a fact Alfie personally found
somewhat of a tenuous claim:

> "Whenever I flew in a Southampton we never knew what was going
> to happen next. It made life rather exciting, if unpredictable. Part
> of the problem stemmed from the fact that the engines' radiators
> had no covers, and the engineers were forever plugging leaks with
> chewing gum (the universal adhesive!). The sparking plugs also
> needed to be regularly cleaned, or else the engines would misfire with
> impressively noisy results. Indeed if I have one overriding memory
> of the Supermarine Southampton, it is the noise. There was no such
> thing as sound proofing in those days, and the poor pilots sat in a
> cockpit that was open to the elements that only added to the noise.
>
> "It was also remarkably cold. Although we were kitted out in

submarine sweaters and the hugely bulky Sidcot suits, the cold always managed to penetrate every layer. On my hands I wore gloves over silk inners, but had to take both the gloves and the inners off to operate the wireless set. Sometimes, quite literally, I lost all feeling in my hands, to the extent that operating the morse key became painful."

Squadron life fell into a typical peacetime routine that was both comfortable and enjoyable. The crews spent time on fighter affiliation exercises where the RAF's latest fighter aircraft (usually Bristol Bulldogs of 29 or 56 Squadrons) would conduct practice interceptions and the Southamptons would attempt to fend them off. (The Southampton was armed with three Lewis machine guns in the bows and amidships.) They went on night-reconnaissance and shadowing exercises with the battleships, *Nelson* and *Rodney* and the Home Fleet, and hunted for the occasional submarine:

"Our main purpose was, of course, to locate enemy shipping or submarines, and having done so, to whistle up the bombers and torpedo squadrons to make an attack. In all of these exercises I saw very little for I was glued to my set in case something should go wrong, and had only the very tiniest of small portholes from which to see. Communication with my fellow crew was difficult, although we did by then have one of the early intercom systems and so no one crew member was totally isolated."

One duty that had a particular poignancy for them all was when they were called upon to search for a missing vessel or aircraft in distress. The boat's long range and duration meant they could cover many miles of sea, but trying to spot the debris from a ship or a life raft bobbing about in the swirling grey was an almost impossible task, and so it was one afternoon when they set off to hunt for a missing Fairey IIIF seaplane. Despite their very best efforts, nothing was ever found of either the aircraft or its crew, and both are assumed to have gone to a watery grave.

———————

The highlight of every year was the annual air-firing and bombing practice that usually took place in the early summer. In the summer of 1933, the squadron had been to Lough Neagh in Northern Ireland and then proceeded to Londonderry in tandem with an Italian transatlantic flight, of twenty-four seaplanes, visiting Lough Foyle.

Various senior personnel were flown in squadron aircraft: Air Marshal Sir Robert

Clark-Hall CMG, DSO (who at the time was the AOC Coastal Area and was later knighted); Signor Grandi (the Italian ambassador); the Italian finance minister (the head of the Italian delegation to the world economic conference); General Pellegrine; and Lieutenant Colonel Cagna.

The most significant passenger, however, was General Italo Balbo, then a world-famous aviator whose air tactics would later give rise to the massed 'Balbo formations'. (Balbo would later have the misfortune of being shot down and killed by his own side over Tobruk in 1940.)

Alfie's first annual air-firing and bombing practice was at Newport near St Andrews, the squadron personnel being based at RAF Leuchars. They dropped their bombs (the Southampton could carry around 1,100 pounds of bombs) on a range located at the end of the Forth. The following year they went there again, but this time under the watchful eye of a new commanding officer. Wigglesworth had moved on, and handed command to Squadron Leader John Breakey DFC*. Breakey was as different to Wigglesworth as Wigglesworth had been to Turner.

The men would often hear rumours on a squadron about the movement of officers, and by the time Breakey arrived, Alfie already had a good idea of the calibre of man the squadron was getting. Like Wigglesworth he had been an ace pilot in the First World War, but unlike Wigglesworth had flown fighters. Indeed Breakey, a Yorkshireman, was an 'ace' in every sense, having been credited with shooting down nine German aircraft in the First World War, and serving as a flying officer in Russia in 1919. He seemed considerably younger than the 'old man' (he was in fact thirty-six) and was instantly popular.

Breakey was not the only interesting character to serve on the squadron during Alfie's time at 201. Among the officers posted to Calshot in early 1934 was a young flying officer by the name of Charles Boyce. He had been posted in from another flying-boat squadron, 210, and was soon after promoted flight lieutenant as one of the flight commanders. Boyce's fast-track promotion continued and he would later become the senior air staff officer (SASO) at 8 Group, Pathfinder Force (PFF).

---

*Later Air Vice-Marshal J D Breakey CB, CBE, DFC & Bar, AOC Malaya 1945-50 and AOC 21 Group Training Command.

Another noteworthy contemporary, albeit another officer, was Pilot Officer Patrick Dunn who would later rise to the rank of air marshal and retire as Sir Patrick Hunter Dunn KBE, CB, DFC. He was posted in at the same time as Flight Lieutenant John McFarlane MC AFC (later group captain OBE).

Towards the end of his eighteen-month stint with 201 Squadron Alfie was due to be posted to India, but fate stepped in:

> "As a Brat I had signed up to twelve years service with a commitment to five of those years being service overseas, and I was very much looking forward to it. But just before we left I began to feel rather unwell: my mouth was dry, I had difficulty swallowing, and my joints were beginning to ache. Reporting to the sick bay, the MO felt the sides of my face where the glands had clearly swollen and diagnosed mumps. This was my first real set-back since joining the RAF. Until then, everything had gone as intended but now I found myself left at home while the rest of the squadron shipped overseas. I felt rather sorry for myself as I lay in bed waiting for my illness to subside.
>
> "It was a strange feeling, being on a base when all of your crewmates had gone, until one day a notice appeared on the board asking for volunteers to join the Singapore Delivery Flight. I had no idea what that actually was, but quickly found out that it was responsible for ferrying new aircraft to squadron bases in the East. This was just the opportunity I was looking for. With my health now fully recovered, I immediately put my name down. After the shortest of interviews I was selected, and posted soon after to Felixstowe."

Reporting to the Singapore Delivery Flight Alfie was instructed to head down to Woolston to pick up a new boat from the Supermarine Aviation Works – a Supermarine Scapa.

When Alfie first clapped eyes on the Scapa he couldn't see much difference in the new design to the old Southamptons he had been flying, other than the fact it had twin fins and rudders rather than three. Apart from that it seemed to be the same size and shape, and the basic layout was the same. It did not come as a surprise, therefore, to discover that the Scapa had been originally designated the Southampton IV. But on closer inspection, the designer (none other than the mercurial R J Mitchell) had given the boat a complete overhaul: the centre section had been re-designed to be more aerodynamic, and the engines were mounted differently. Whereas the Southampton's twin Lions had been mounted mid way between the upper and lower mainplanes, the Scapa had its engines and their cowlings faired smoothly into the upper wings. The engines themselves were different: the Lions had been replaced by more powerful Rolls-Royce Kestrels, giving her a top speed of 137 mph at sea level and more superior performance all round. The hull had also been redesigned with straighter sides, thus giving the crew more room inside.★

> "The new aircraft was particularly robust. We appreciated this when we witnessed her undergoing a 'shakedown'. Apparently this happened to all flying boats at Supermarine at this time. The boat was effectively winched up on a crane to a specified height and then dropped! They seemed satisfied with the results, and given that the boat hadn't fallen apart, we were then cleared to take her away! Before we went, however, some of the engineers at the works were keen to show us their latest creation. We were taken into one of the sheds and caught sight, for the first time, of an aircraft that would later go on to achieve world-wide fame. Although the aircraft was only a half-sized model, it was unmistakably a Spitfire."

The crew eventually left Supermarine and flew its Scapa down to Mount Batten (Plymouth) to take on supplies. They then set off for Alexandria, via a route that would first take them over the Bay of Biscay to Bordeaux. It was, Alfie recalled, a beautiful day, and looking out through his tiny porthole into the bay he observed that the sea had a perfect sheen, and the surface was glistening in the sunlight. He remembers it so clearly because he was soon after shaken from his idyllic reverie by the not so dreamlike smell of petrol:

> "I reported the fact to the skipper, Flight Lieutenant W G A 'Abie' Abrams, and sure enough there was a broken fuel pipe feeding the port engine.
>
> "Abrams seemed unperturbed by the difficulty. He was one of those pilots who never seemed to get into a flap. Most of us aircrew could tell you what they thought of the men who flew them. They will understand what I mean if I said that with Abrams you always felt 'safe'. You knew you were in safe hands. He was confident, but not over-confident. He was young, but somehow very experienced. He could also be quite an eccentric: he had a little white dog that he used

---

★The prototype Scapa was first flown by test pilot 'Mutt' Summers on July 8, 1932. Interestingly, only fifteen Scapas were ever built.

to bring out with him on parade, and was very keen on sport, especially golf. He once attempted to play hockey and I simply remember him wrapping his stick around the neck of one of our opponents!

"Anyhow, Abrams said that he would land to allow the fitter an opportunity to fix a repair. Clearly since we were coming down in the sea I needed to transmit a 'distress' signal to base which I did using the 600 meter band (the distress frequency). I transmitted our position ('260 Bell Island 16' – funny how I can still remember that seventy years after the event!) and made contact with two ships to come to our aid if need be. I also made contact with the squadron CO at Mount Batten on high frequency.

"The wireless set in those day comprised a fixed aerial and a trailing (100ft) aerial, and I was still winding in the trailing aerial when the aircraft landed, with what seemed like half the Bay of Biscay coming up through the aerial chute giving me a good soaking!"

The fitter managed to effect a repair to the fuel pipe, and within thirty minutes they were under way, the pilot hitting three waves before the aircraft finally struggled into the sky. Both pilots kept a watchful eye on the gauges and all seemed in order. The smell of petrol also quickly disappeared.

"From Bordeaux we flew to Marseille and attempted to reach Malta before finally settling for Tunisia. We landed at a French airfield but that in itself proved difficult, as they did not allow the use of wireless three miles from the base. After an overnight stay, we proceeded from Tunisia and eventually made landfall in Alexandria and handed over our Scapa to 202 Squadron.

"That might have been the end of that particular story but during the incident over the Bay of Biscay, I had somehow managed to lose the weight off the end of the trailing aerial. The air force, being as it was in those days, did not like us to lose any of its equipment without a full explanation and demanded an enquiry.

The weight was categorised as a 'B' store meaning that you could not be given a new one, unless you handed in the old one first. I am not quite sure how, and I certainly didn't ask, but Flight Lieutenant Abrams soon had everything sorted, and after a short stay with the chaps at 202 Squadron we learned that we would be returning by sea. In our civilian clothes, we spent a thoroughly glorious ten-day cruise home on the 64,000-ton RMS *Strathaird*."

201 Squadron was re-equipped with the Saunders-Roe London flying boat in April 1936.

("As a footnote to this story – two weeks after we left we heard that 'our' aircraft had collided with the stern of a destroyer and was written off.")

The flying-boat squadrons of the RAF in the 1930s operated a number of different types: Alfie had experience of the Southampton and the Scapa, both from Supermarine. He also remembers flying the Saunders-Roe London. The other major manufacturer at that time, and Supermarine's greatest rival, was Short Brothers. Short had designed a long series of biplane flying boats, among them the Calcutta and the Rangoon. Its most famous flying boat, the Short Sunderland, was yet to appear, but its immediate predecessor – and the next aircraft Alfie was detailed to deliver – was the Short Singapore III.

A little history of the development of the Singapore III might be in order. The original Singapore (the Singapore I) had been designed in 1926, and as a type it had achieved fame when one of the first aircraft had been loaned to the great Sir Alan Cobham for his acclaimed 23,000-mile flight around Africa in 1927-8. A second mark of Singapore (the Singapore II) was designed but never went into production, leaving the final variant, the Singapore III, which first entered service in April 1935.

The twin-engined Singapore III also used a version of the Rolls-Royce Kestrels that powered the Supermarine Scapa, giving her a top speed of 145 mph at 2,000ft. Like the Southampton, she was armed with three Lewis machine guns but could carry twice the weight (around 2,000 pounds) of bombs. The Singapore IIIs were manufactured in five production batches, the third of which were coded K6907 to K6922. Alfie's next instruction was to pick up K6910 (call sign GEZ 6K) from Short's manufacturing works at Rochester in Kent, and deliver her to 205 (FB) Squadron in Singapore.

"For this trip we had a different crew. Abrams was once again in the pilot's seat, but sitting alongside him as second pilot/engineer was Sergeant Pat Searle. Sergeant pilots were unusual in the RAF because it was always assumed that flying was the preserve of the officer classes, but Pat was superb. Like me he had been at Halton, and prior to being on flying boats I believe he had been on a fighter squadron, flying one of the last of the RAF's bi-plane fighters. Our engineer for this trip was Corporal 'Rev' Carter who was reckoned to be one of the best at his trade, and our fitter was another corporal, Bill Williams. Bill, who gloried under the nickname of 'Pisser', was one of the best-known airframe fitters in flying boats who could make things and fix problems that nobody else could. All in all we were in safe hands.

"It was a long haul from the Short works in Rochester to Singapore that we undertook in several stages, setting off on the morning of April 29. Pat's wife came to wave us off, a fact I remember because she was also there, three weeks later, to greet our arrival. We flew first to Mount Batten and then onwards to Gibraltar, a trip of ten hours and twenty minutes. The Spanish civil war was on and we were not allowed to overfly Spain. The aircraft only had a cruising speed of ninety knots. We had to go round Portugal, Cape Finisterre and into Gib. We were exhausted when we arrived."

After an overnight stay at Gibraltar they went to Malta, Aboukir (on the Mediterranean coast of Egypt), Habbaniya and onward to Karachi (Pakistan).

At Karachi, their otherwise-reliable boat developed a fault in one of the engines, and this meant a short delay. It developed a leak, and they spent a week waiting for a new cylinder block to arrive at the airport. With the repairs made, they continued their onward journey to Islamabad, Calcutta (Merguy) and thence to Seletar on the north-east coast of the island of Singapore, a leisurely journey of more than 8,000 miles. They arrived at 1.45pm local time.

"There was little real excitement along the way and, other than the engine repair, our boat performed splendidly. Wherever possible we landed at known RAF mooring places: there were buoys, for example, in Alexandria, Aboukir, and Habbaniya, but in Karachi and Merguy we were obliged to use civilian moorings operated by the local coastguard. I never had any trouble connecting with the RAF on their wavelengths or communicating with the civilian radio stations on theirs. It was always important to let everyone know where you were, and I was never out of communication with land.

"We were always trained how to communicate with civilian systems and airwaves; we would notify them in advance if possible of our route and kept communication in what was called the Q Code – a code of three letters that provided all sorts of information including all necessary frequencies, weather forecasts en route and the condition of the station we were visiting. If we needed a comfort break then I would send Q1P so that they would know I would be off air for a little while.

"The only ordeal on the trip was that every night, after we landed, one of us was obliged to sleep on the boat, leaving the others to explore the local hospitality. Our crew pay in 1936 was one and six, and we received an extra shilling for staying with the boat. I seemed to recall that 'Pisser' was never that keen, so I volunteered to take his watch for the extra cash!"

The grateful recipient of their boat was 205 Squadron, a unit that had been out in the Far East since 1929 and had, until very recently, been equipped with Southamptons. It was at that time under the command of Squadron Leader K B Lloyd. Their boat, and that of K6911, both arrived in Seletar on May 22, 1936 – three days behind schedule – a fact recorded in the squadron's ORB:

'K6910 and K6911 arrived by air from the United Kingdom to bring
the squadron up to establishment of six aircraft.'

Having completed their trip, they half expected to be posted home but instead found themselves officially posted to the squadron along with the second crew.

The two years Alfie spent in Singapore were some of the happiest in his life. It was a haven of pleasure:

"If you can imagine, I was only twenty-one years of age, footloose and fancy free. I was well paid (thirty-nine bob a week), well fed and well looked after. The food – which was all rather exotic compared to what we had been used to – was well cooked and in plentiful supply.

"RAF Seletar was a permanent station, and still very new. It had been established as an airfield, flying boat and naval base to defend one of the British Empire's most distant territories. As such it was very well equipped. We lived in an earthquake-proof accommodation block (Block F) that was surrounded by trenches that were six feet deep to cope with the monsoon. These 'sumatras', as the locals called them, were spectacular to experience: the sky would literally turn black as night, and the flashes of lightening and rolls of thunder would soon after be joined by a torrential downfall of rain of almost biblical proportions. And then as quickly as the storm had come, it was gone: the sun would be shining and the birds would once again be screeching and calling in the trees. Unlike a storm in England, however, the rain was warm, and once it had stopped, any surface water would quickly evaporate as though it had all happened in your imagination. It was a very surreal experience.

"Our pay was such that there was little we could not afford if we wanted it. There were eight Singapore dollars and twenty cents to the pound; a silk shirt would cost you one dollar or you could spend three dollars on a pair of silk pyjamas. On our days off, we would head north to Penang, where there was a dance hall that proved especially popular with the men."

It was not all fun of course; there was still lots of work for Alfie and his colleagues to do:

"The boats had to be inspected every ten hours and we were grounded, of course, while these were done. More detailed checks were required every twenty and forty hours and then the big one at 120 hours going through the life of the aircraft."

The RAF was responsible for a vast territory that fell within their sphere of operations. The Far Eastern Command stretched from Hong Kong and Borneo in the east, to Siam (as it was then called) and Burma in the north. A couple of months after their arrival, and having settled in nicely, they were called upon to take a rather special flight in the company of a number of senior dignitaries. The ORB for August 17, 1936 states simply:

'K6910 commenced cruise to Darwin, Australia via Batavia, Sourabaya, Koepang with Dr Earl Page* [sic], Deputy Prime Minister and AOC.'

---

*Sir Earle Page later became prime minister of Australia for only twenty days, between April 7, 1939 and April 26, 1939. He was deputy prime minister twice, between 1923-1929, and then again between 1934-1939. He died in 1961.

Earle Page, who as well as being deputy prime minister was also the minister for commerce, had come to Singapore, according to contemporary newspaper reports, to discuss the possibility of increasing trade between Australia and Malaya. He was also there to inspect the progress being made in the construction of the Singapore naval base in which the Australians had a vested interest. Prior to arriving on the island, he had been in London, discussing with British military, naval and air authorities 'the closer co-ordination of Imperial defence plans in the Pacific and Far East, with special reference to Singapore'. (*The Straits Times*, August 14, 1936).

"The 'cruise' as the ORB calls it, took us to Port Darwin via the Dutch East Indies. When we did finally make Darwin, we were put up in a small red-dust village with a single hotel and a hitching post for horses that made it look like something out of the Wild West. There was a sign above the main bar that read simply: 'Cancel your allotment or die of thirst.' We later spent a week at Port Moresby before returning to Seletar. We had covered more than 5,000 miles in the course of ten days, and were gratified to see the trip later described in official terms as 'highly successful and without incident'. It was also described as one of the most important long-distance cruises ever undertaken by an RAF unit.

"A few weeks later and we were one of two flying boats (the other flown by Squadron Leader Cyril Riccard) to escort the AOC and his chief staff officer (Group Captain A H Peck DSO, MC) to Hong Kong, where a conference was being planned with the Chinese leader General Chiang kai-shek. We got as far as Hong Kohe in Indo-China, when a tropical storm began to brew. It was, without question, the most extreme weather we had ever encountered.

"It was not only the rain that was the issue, albeit that it reduced visibility to only a few hundred feet, but rather the winds, which meant we made little headway and were being blown all over the sky. Climbing above it was impossible – we simply did not have the power and the winds were too strong – and there was a danger too in flying too close to the sea. We battled on for almost four hours and I was in wireless communication with Seletar throughout. Since we were still relative newcomers to the region, we were given orders to turn back. Even this was easier said than done, but soon after, and with much skill on the part of our pilot, we effected a landing at Kan-Ranh Bay in Annam. It was a relief to be down in one piece – a great testament to the ruggedness of our Singapore IIIs and to the cool head of Abrams. Riccard, who was more familiar with the route, flew on and safely made landfall in Hong Kong. We followed the next day, by which time the storm had subsided."

Another ORB entry for October 10, 1936 gives a clue as to the main purpose of having a flying-boat squadron in the Far East:

'K6910 and K6911 took part in combined exercises in defence of Singapore against attack. Machines spotted and shadowed HMS *Terror* in preparation for attack on it by torpedo bombers.'

Alfie enjoyed these exercises immensely, tracking the unmistakable lines of a warship that was obviously of first war vintage, with her two fifteen-inch guns mounted in a central turret*. They shared their home at Seletar with 36 and 100 Squadrons, both of which were equipped with Vickers Vildebeest torpedo bombers. The Vildebeest looked out of date even when it was new, and they were still on the squadrons' strength when the Japanese invaded five years later!

"Our principal role was as a reconnaissance aircraft, but we did not only keep an eye out for potential invaders. We were also called upon to help maintain law and order, the military working closely in co-operation (as they do today) with HM Customs. Smuggling of booze and cigarettes was big business, and we would spot for boats that were suspicious by their actions or their location. It would then be my job to report their position and keep watch until a surface vessel could reach them. It was rarely rewarding, the phrase 'unremunerative search' appearing regularly in reports of the time.

"Pirates were a very real problem, especially along the Malayan coast, and we would also act as an air ambulance for local workers if they fell ill. We would mark them in our log books as 'flights of mercy'. Every month we would fly the mail to the White Rajah in Sarawak, Sir Robert Brooke, and on other occasions would cruise up and down the coast of British North Borneo to test the wireless stations. This used to make me smile because they probably knew more about wireless than I did!"

---

*HMS *Terror* was later sunk in Derna, Libya, after a sustained attack by Junkers 88 bombers.

A change in squadron command occurred in November 1936 with the arrival of Squadron Leader Alick Stevens and departure of Squadron Leader Lloyd two weeks later. This left Alfie's own skipper, Flight Lieutenant Abrams, as next in seniority, and Abrams did indeed take command of the squadron, albeit temporarily, when Stevens fell sick (Stevens was eventually invalided home). Abrams' elevation did not last long, however, for on January 8, 1937, Squadron Leader A W Bates was attached to take temporary command from 230 (FB) Squadron. This latter unit and its Singapore IIIs had only just arrived in Seletar to bolster their strength. They were a welcome addition to share the load.

The change in squadron command coincided with promotions at a higher level and the arrival of a new flying-boat squadron to further strengthen their numbers. This included specifically the appointment of a new air officer commanding, Far Eastern Air Force, Air Commodore Arthur Tedder, who arrived on the P&O Liner *Naldera* on November 6. Three of the squadron's boats (as well as a number of Vildebeest and army co-operation Hawker Audax aircraft) flew out to escort the liner from the Sultan Shoal buoy to the entrance of Keppel Harbour. His coming was followed soon after by the arrival of five flying boats of 230 (FB) Squadron at Seletar.

Tedder, a World War I veteran and squadron commander, was a forceful personality who made it clear from the start that his style of command would be very different from that of his predecessor (Air Commodore Sydney Smith). He abhorred the pomp and ceremony that went with his appointment, but understood too the need to maintain a pretence of calm and authority, even if it would sometimes frustrate him. His main focus was around training and preparedness for war. He was especially keen on ensuring closer co-operation between the air force and the navy, and this is probably why the frequency of combined exercises increased noticeably in the first few months of his arrival.

The year started, for example, with a combined operation in which boats from Alfie's squadron and 230 'co-operated' in the search for and shadowing of four Royal Navy destroyers:

> "This was tiring work that tested our endurance to the limit. Even more exhausting was a major combined exercise a few weeks later, on February 2, the largest of its kind ever undertaken in the region. It was conducted with the purpose of testing Singapore's defences from attack by an imaginary foe. It did not take much imagination, however, to work out who that foe was expected to be, since the Japanese had been agitating in the region for some time. The exercise had been much anticipated, and we were divided into 'Blueland' (for the enemy) and 'Redland' (to denote friendly forces). A number of

squadrons flew in from India and Iraq to bolster our defences, and
in an attempt to make the exercise as realistic as possible."

This particular exercise got off to a terrible start. One of the squadron's boats crashed on take-off into the Straits of Johor in the early dawn, and the second pilot (Pilot Officer Robert Blair) was killed. He was taken from the general hospital to the cemetery and buried with full military honours two days later. He had only been with them since September, and was a reminder of the dangers of flying, even when there was nobody shooting real bullets.

Notwithstanding their own personal tragedy, the exercise, which lasted until February 4, was deemed a tremendous success. Needless to say that 'Redland' won easily, and within two days the invading forces had been despatched with a metaphorical bloody nose and much celebration on Alfie's part.

The true success or otherwise of the exercise, of course, Alfie never knew. They had only their own squadron debriefing and the pages of *The Straits Times* to go by, and the newspaper was gushing in its praise. However, what did actually happen when 'Blueland' attacked is one for the history books.

Anti-submarine patrols in restricted waters were flown on February 11, 13, 16, 19 and 24, before Alfie's own boat and crew was detailed to fly the AOC and a number of army, navy and air force staff officers to a conference to discuss the defence of Penang. They did not return until the first week of March, by which stage they had a new officer commanding, Wing Commander Percy Maitland MVO, AFC*. Maitland was another ex-airship type and an expert in navigation. His fame preceded him for some time earlier he had taken part in a record-breaking long-distance flight to Australia, and so there was quite a stir when he called the squadron together and they saw him for the first time. He also brought with him a party of fitter IIs and mates to replace a number who had recently been posted home.

———————

Tedder's passion for training probably explains why they spent the next few months experimenting in the use of the squadron's flying boats, turning them from reconnaissance into attack aircraft:

———————

* Later Air Vice-Marshal Percy Maitland CB, CBE, MVO, AFC AOC 93 (OTU) Group, 1942-43.

"One of our boats took part in an anti-submarine patrol, but rather than simply spotting for submarines on the surface and calling in the bombers, this time we were expected to attack the submarine ourselves. The secret was in attempting to get within range of the sub without being seen and execute a surprise attack. It was of course easier said than done, but I would like to think that some of our squadron's experiments helped later flying-boat crews to perfect the art."

As well as wanting to bring his command up to the mark, Tedder was also keen to seek new sites for his flying-boat and seaplane squadrons, and various boats were sent out to explore the areas of Kuala Selangor and Kuantan to find suitable locations. Two boats were also despatched to Batavia to take part in the Coronation celebrations and as a gesture of goodwill to the British community in the region. This latter mission was headed by the squadron's new officer commanding:

"We were ourselves called upon to fly to Borneo to inspect a new landing ground, but while we were there we suffered problems with one of our engines. Although our [engineer] tried everything he could, including chewing gum, it was clear that the engine was past redemption and I was obliged to send word for a new engine to be brought out to us at Kuching (the capital of Sarawak. Kuching is Malay for 'many cats' and there were thousands of them). The delay had its plus points, however, for it allowed us some time off to trek into the hills where my abiding memories are of the wild Orangutan and Proboscis monkeys with their comedy noses who would stare at us from out of the jungle as if we were the strange ones."

The squadron's Singapore IIIs suffered the air force equivalent of a product recall notice in July, when a serious and potentially-dangerous fault was found with the control cables that needed modification. The result was that all of their boats were placed as 'unserviceable' (u/s) until the fault could be rectified. The event coincided with news that Alfie's pilot had been promoted squadron leader, which gave cause for modest celebration. (The AOC also received confirmation of his promotion to air vice-marshal.)

"Although we did not think it at the time, the difficulties we were beginning to experience served only to highlight the inadequacies of our equipment in defending what was considered to be one of the most important strategic outposts in the Empire. It took more than two months before our OC was able to report his squadron as being once again 100 per cent operational, during which time 205 had also been renamed 205 (General Reconnaissance) Squadron, thus losing our 'flying boat' identity.

"Once our boats had been modified, we began flying again and regularly co-operated not only with our own Royal Navy vessels but also ships from the Royal Australian Navy, notably the heavy cruiser, HMAS *Canberra*. Among the exercises now being practiced was to maintain twenty-four-hour watch over a target vessel, with the duties being shared between three of our boats. Wireless transmission was of course crucial to achieving success, and on more than one occasion wireless failure conspired to let the side down."

At the beginning of 1938, two flying boats – 6911 and Alfie's own 6910 – embarked on a two-week cruise to Rangoon. The journey plotted took them via Penang, Victoria Point and Merguy, conveying the AOC, a Squadron Leader Vines, and Mr Hallas – an engineer within the Works Directorate – to Burma. The AOC kept Alfie busy. He had a daughter to whom he was clearly devoted. At every stop-over, he would hand Alfie a foolscap sheet of paper with a series of messages to send to her. Their business concluded they did not leave Rangoon to return to Seletar until January 14 with further passengers, among them the inspector general of the RAF, Air Marshal Sir Edward Ellington GCB, CMG, OBE. He was making an inspection tour of RAF stations in the Far East.

Another of Tedder's showpiece combined exercises commenced on February 2 at midday. More than 10,000 men, twenty-five warships and 120 aircraft took part, and it was again a success, at least officially. In fact, it was an unmitigated disaster. On successive nights, the attacking carrier (HMS *Eagle*) closed to within 135 miles of Redland and its bombers hit all targets unopposed:

"For our own part, we were one of the first boats to take off on the first day in company with 6911 to undertake a sector search to a depth of 210 miles from Seletar. Despite our best efforts we failed to sight a single ship, returning home after a flight of almost six-and-a-half hours. We took off again early the next morning to escort a torpedo-bomber squadron that was attempting to attack HMS *Eagle*, and again on the morning of the 4th for further reconnaissance."

In all, over the four days, the squadron aircraft flew more than sixty-two hours, and nearly sixteen hours were accredited to Alfie's own aircraft and crew. It was disappointing, however, to read later in the pages of the *Straits Times* the editor of the *Aeroplane*, C G Grey, being quoted as describing Singapore's defences as 'the laughing stock of any intelligent Asiatic'.

To add insult to injury, ten days later on February 14 they were one of three boats detailed to take part in a flypast of the squadron at Singapore to celebrate the official opening of the new dry dock and naval base. It was a rather splendid pageant, though they might have thought differently had they known that the occasion was attended by the Japanese consul-general!

It was, as it happens, one of Alfie's last flights with 205 Squadron. He had seen the Air Ministry Order (AMO) looking for aircrew to volunteer for training as observers in preparation for what seemed like an inevitable war with Germany:

> "Given my experience, and a desire to enhance both my chances of promotion and my pay cheque, I put my name down on the list and soon after found myself in front of the AOC for interview. I recall little of what was said, save for the fact that Tedder seemed to be aware of my interest in hockey (I was in charge of the Seletar hockey team) and that as long as I was fit, then I was good for further training. I had kept my nose clean, and no doubt had a good report from 'Abie'.
>
> "Tedder did ask me my ambition, and I replied that I wanted ultimately to be a pilot, but was happy to be an observer first and work my way up. At that time there was a suggestion that observer training was a route to further advancement, but of course I later discovered, as hundreds after me also found, that this was somewhat disingenuous. Within a few days I was given passage for the long journey home."

A new stage in Alfie's air force career was about to begin, and one that would have far-reaching consequences.

CHAPTER TWO
——CHANGING DIRECTIONS——

The trip home on the 15,000-ton SS *Corfu* was far from a pleasure cruise as the ship rolled from side to side virtually all of the way back to 'Blighty'. There were twelve in all coming home: nine to train as observers and three as pilots. It took them three weeks to sail via Bombay, through the Suez Canal and into the Mediterranean to Alexandria, and thence onwards to the UK having called in at Malta and Gibraltar along the way.

> "My family were pleased to see me, though what they quite made of me having been away for so long with nothing but the occasional airmail letter and postcard is difficult to imagine. I was given a short period of leave before heading north to commence a three-month air observer's course at North Coates Fitties near Grimsby."

It was in December 1935 that the Air Ministry announced the formation of the Air Observers School (AOS) at North Coates Fitties to commence January 1, 1936. The official notice reads that: 'The school will undertake the conduct of courses for: Air observers; Air gunners; Telegraphist air gunners.' It was placed under the command of the AOC Inland Area for administration and the AOC Armament Group for training.

Air observers were expected to have a range of different skills. These in short may have been defined as being to undertake any task the pilot requested! Aircraft had become more sophisticated over time, requiring the knowledge and skills of aircrew to increase commensurately. They would, of course, become even more sophisticated over the next few years with the entry into service of the first four-engined bombers, but for now the task of observer, navigator, bomb aimer, and occasional air gunner were denoted by one man wearing a single half wing brevet, the 'flying arsehole' as they liked to call it.

Alfie's own training commenced in March 1938, a somewhat historic period in the road towards ultimate war. British newspapers were reporting the annexation of Austria (the so-called '*Anschluss*') by the German Führer, Adolf Hitler, and the implications to peace in Europe. In the weeks that followed there was more worrying news as Hitler laid claim to the Sudetenland (an area of Czechoslovakia inhabited primarily by German-speaking Czechs) and the rest of Europe stood idly by. It added a new urgency to Alfie's training.

"As it was, I was one of about sixty trainee air observers on the course and our training was somewhat truncated. This was not because war was so imminent or that they were in any rush to get rid of me, but rather because of my proficiency in some of the areas in which we were being instructed.

"Wireless instruction, for example, was not necessary; indeed I think I could have taught the instructors a thing or two! I had learned some navigation at Greenwich that also proved handy.

"I had also already received some training in air gunnery. One of the exercises that we had to master was the ability to strip a Vickers 'K' machine gun (the chosen weapon of the moment) blindfolded, and be able to put it back together again, all within five minutes. I seemed to be quite good at air gunnery, achieving good marks in the final exams. Photography similarly came naturally.

"There was one amusing story of a fellow pupil named 'Dippy' Diprose. Dippy was almost always in the sick bay, but determined to finish the course, come what may. One afternoon he was in the air, practice firing at a drogue. (A drogue was like a windsock towed behind an aircraft as a target for use in air-to-air firing exercises.) Almost immediately after loosing off a burst, Dippy began thumping his instructor pilot on the back, urgently pointing to the ground. It seemed clear from his wild gesticulating that there was a problem, so the pilot dutifully stuck the nose down and headed for mother earth as quickly as he could. No sooner had they landed then the pilot asked Dippy what was wrong. 'There's nothing wrong,' the pupil replied. 'I just wanted to see if any of my bullets had hit the target!'

"Some parts of the course were more demanding than others.

Although I quite took to navigation, and was considered satisfactory, I challenge anyone to be able to map read at low level in an open cockpit Westland Wallace – a two-seat general purpose biplane that served as our principal airborne trainer alongside the ubiquitous Avro Anson. For one thing, the ground simply passed by too quickly, and for another my maps kept blowing out of the cockpit!

"Without doubt my weakest subject was air bombing, and at the time I rather fancied I might fail that part of the course. As it happened, my results proved to be no better or worse than the next, and given the rather low-technology bombsight we were using at the time, I would be surprised if anyone hit anything on purpose."

It seemed that no sooner had Alfie's course started that it was over, and all of the successful pupils were paraded in front of the officer commanding (Wing Commander Geoffrey Pidcock) to be given their air observers brevets. Alfie was also promoted, being able to sew on his hard-earned corporal's stripes.

"I say that they were hard earned for a very good reason. My training at North Coates Fitties coincided with the RAF's drive for sergeant observers on direct entry. This meant that people like me, with several years' service behind us, suddenly found ourselves outranked by men with no service experience whatsoever. Although the situation was soon rectified for aircrew (we were promised that we would be promoted sergeant within six months) I know that it was an issue that continued to rankle many of the ground crew and with some justification. It was also something that caused issues in the prison camps later."

Alfie's promotion, and his new qualification, was followed by the inevitable wait for a posting. He had become good friends during this time with a fellow 'regular', Alex Logan*, and they were both keen to see where they would be sent.

---

*Flying over Belgium on May 25, 1940, Alex was part of a crew skippered by Flying Officer Eric Nind when their aircraft was hit by ground fire. Alex was severely wounded in the leg by an explosive bullet, and in the end had to have his leg amputated. Eric Nind later went on to become a wing commander and win the DFC with Pathfinder Force. Logan became a squadron leader station engineer in PFF.

"I had hoped to be sent back to flying boats, but the RAF had other ideas. Observers were required for the bombing and reconnaissance squadrons, and so in June 1938 Alex and I found ourselves with our kit bags and a few bob between us at a railway station near Oxford, waiting to cadge a lift to RAF Upper Heyford and our new home, 57 (Reconnaissance) Squadron."

There had been an RAF presence at Upper Heyford since 1916. It had been a training base for new pilots and gunners. Located in the pretty Oxfordshire countryside, not far from the historic town of Bicester, its grass airfield had originally been semi-enclosed by a large forest of trees, which must have made it interesting for any aircraft finding itself in trouble!

It was some time after the First World War, in the late 1920s, that the first bomber squadrons began arriving at Upper Heyford, although it continued to train pupil students from the Oxford University Air Squadron. By the time he arrived, Upper Heyford was the home base for two squadrons – 18 Squadron and 57 Squadron – which then were part of 70 Wing that in turn was attached to 2 Group, headquartered in Abingdon (it moved to Wyton on the outbreak of war).

Alfie's new squadron had been an early pioneer in bombing and reconnaissance. Formed on June 8, 1916, the squadron crossed to France in December of the same year as a fighter-reconnaissance squadron equipped with FE2ds. The following spring, the unit re-equipped with the impressive De Havilland DH4s, and in June moved to the Ypres sector to begin long-distance reconnaissance, bombing and photography operations, sometimes deep into enemy territory.

Results were impressive, and further improved with the addition of oxygen breathing apparatus and negative-lens bombsights, and by the end of the war the squadron had shot down 166 enemy aircraft, dropped 285 tons of bombs, exposed more than 22,000 photographic plates and completed almost 200 successful reconnaissance sorties.

Like many units in the years that followed the war, 57 Squadron was soon after disbanded and then reformed in 1931 under the command of Squadron Leader H G Bowen MBE as a single-engined day-bomber squadron flying the famous Hawker Hart. In the squadron's hands, the Hart proved to be one of the most adaptable biplanes ever to enter service and it was not until May 1936 that the unit was subsequently re-equipped with the Hart's successor, the Hawker Hind. The Hind was a beautiful aeroplane, both to look at and to fly, but was only ever intended as an interim measure. The age of the biplane was quickly passing, and by the time of Alfie's arrival, the Hinds had themselves been replaced by the Bristol Blenheim Mark I, the first aircraft having been collected from the manufacturers on March 25. (The last Hind was allocated to another squadron on May 19.)

The Bristol Blenheim was a very different aircraft in every sense. To begin with, it had started life as a private venture – the Type 135 cabin monoplane – designed by Frank Barnwell in 1933. So revolutionary was its design that it attracted the attention of the press baron, Lord Rothermere, who in 1934 ordered a Mercury-engined version for his own use as part of a campaign to popularise commercial aviation.

The aircraft first flew in April 1935 and similarly caused a stir within the Air Ministry on account of its comparatively high performance, including a top speed that made it faster than any RAF fighter then in service! Lord Rothermere presented the aircraft (named 'Britain First') to the nation for evaluation as a bomber and in early 1936 the modified design was designated the Blenheim Mark I. The first unit to receive the type was 114 Squadron in March 1937.

The early Blenheims were instantly recognisable for their angular perspex nose section that only just extended beyond the propeller blades. With its crew of three, the light bomber could comfortably cruise at 200mph and with throttles fully forward could edge beyond 260mph – a full 80mph faster than the aircraft it replaced. For a small aircraft it had a relatively impressive range, something in the region of 1,125 miles (the Hind was capable only of 430 miles), and could stay aloft for almost six hours – weather and reliability permitting. They were an instant hit with the crews who flew them, notwithstanding a few initial teething problems and issues with serviceability.

When he had first arrived in flying boats in 201 (FB) Squadron, Alfie had been the new boy and had to wait patiently to be allocated to a crew. With 57 Squadron, however, he was an experienced flyer, a veteran with approaching 1,000 hours flying time in his logbook. This time there was no waiting around like a schoolboy hoping to be picked by his peers for a game of five-a-side. This time he was immediately paired with his 'own' pilot – 'Johnnie' Greenleaf – of 'A' Flight:

> "'Johnnie', like me, was a non-commissioned officer (NCO). He had also been, like me, a Halton apprentice, and had joined at exactly the same time and part of the same entry. Unlike me, however, Johnnie had clearly been earmarked as something of a star, and was identified for pilot training – one of the very few of his kind to be so honoured.
>
> "Johnnie had everything going for him: he was a good looking young man of medium build, who was very fit and, as I soon discovered, was very attractive to members of the opposite sex! He was also an extremely-capable pilot, much better than many of the direct-entry pilot officers, with a natural gift for flying to the point that it seemed to be an extension of his being."

Squadron life suited Alfie admirably. His arrival coincided with the squadron's annual-leave period, which allowed him plenty of time to settle in and explore the local hostelries with Alex. Training began again proper in July with a series of live-bombing practices on the ranges at Andover, the squadron experimenting with a range of ordinance from 250-pound general purpose bombs through to the smallest four-pound incendiaries. The RAF also practiced its own version of 'Blitzkrieg', flying close-support trials with various mobile divisions of the army with mixed results. Such periods of activity were not only a trial to aircrew; they were also a test for the men. Each of the Blenheims had a ground crew of at least three: two fitters, one for each engine; and a rigger who looked after the airframe. Each of these three might have a semi-skilled 'mate' to assist them so a light bomber of this period could well pin down the services of nine men at any one time.

When not flying, many of the men would head for Kidlington courtesy of a Morris Minor Tower acquired for Alfie by a nearby motor dealer, Kings of Oxford, for the princely sum of £40. The car allowed Alfie a modicum of freedom from the base which he needed, for he was by now betrothed to Vera Allen, a beautiful young girl he had met while at Calshot. In the autumn of 1938 they had every intention of marrying, but world events got in the way and they were obliged to put any ideas of matrimonial bliss on hold – at least for the time being.

Adolf Hitler, who had caused such a stir earlier in the year in Austria, was agitating again, spurred on no doubt by the toothless response to his aggression from any of the other European leaders. In September, Chamberlain and Deladier – the British and French prime ministers respectively – met the Führer at the now infamous conference in Munich and by doing nothing effectively acquiesced to Hitler's territorial ambitions.

The German leader guaranteed that in return for the Sudetenland, Czechoslovakia would not be attacked. But a guarantee from a liar was not worth the famous piece of paper it was written on, and which Chamberlain flourished with such confidence on his return for 'peace in our time'.

While the politicians argued, Britain was placed on a war footing. At a squadron level, this meant that a signal was received from the Air Ministry cancelling all leave and obliging all airmen to return to their units. Ground crews laboured throughout the next few days to remove the peacetime markings on all aircraft in favour of new, wartime, codes and the men awaited further instructions. At an administrative level, on September 28, 57 Squadron was transferred from 1 Group to 2 Group at Wyton, and a further signal was sent informing the new headquarters that the squadron was deficient in certain key areas, notably rear cockpit turrets and the air gunners to man them. The unit was transferred back to 1 Group command (Abingdon) on October 8.

An uneasy and uncertain peace transcended both the squadron and the country in the coming months. The deficiency in air gunnery identified at the time was soon after corrected, with crews and men (notably wireless ops) sent regularly to Sutton Bridge to increase the numbers of qualified air gunners. Indeed over the winter of 1938/1939, no fewer than fourteen 'new' air gunners were qualified both at Sutton Bridge in Lincolnshire and Warmwell, on the south coast.

On April 5, all leave was once again cancelled and a state of emergency declared. Hitler had broken his promise, occupying Bohemia and Moravia, and war now seemed inevitable. Only now did Chamberlain find the backbone that had been so badly absent at Munich, warning Hitler that if Germany attacked Poland, then Britain would not and could not stand idly by. Meanwhile, RAF squadrons around the UK were once again prepared for war, and squadron establishments increased. At Upper Heyford, 57 Squadron increased its own establishment to one wing commander (commanding), two squadron leaders, two flight lieutenants, and twenty-two other pilots – a total of more than 200 officers and men.

Over the course of the next few days and weeks, further pilots arrived to swell the squadron numbers, some from other squadrons and others from various flying training schools, their training given a new urgency. Spitfires from 'A' Flight of 74 'Tiger' Squadron arrived at Upper Heyford from Hornchurch on April 24 to give the Blenheim crews (and especially the air gunners) some much needed fighter affiliation practice.

The Empire Air Day on May 20 offered the squadron and Alfie a brief but welcome distraction from the preparations for war, and an opportunity to show the British public that they had every reason to feel confident that the RAF had both the aircraft and the men to keep them safe from harm. The gates of the base were thrown open for the day and the two resident squadrons – 57 Squadron and 18 Squadron – gave a display of air drill that thrilled the crowd.

The summer passed rather benignly. Further officers arrived including a former artillery officer, Flight Lieutenant (Captain RA) S S Fielden on June 5, Pilot Officer Frank Campbell Rogers on June 25, and a hat-trick of acting pilot officers on August 5 – Osborne Keedwell, Robert Carr and Frederick Green. (Pilot Officer Keedwell was killed in action on May 12, 1940 while serving with 107 Squadron. Pilot Officer Green went on to end the war as a wing commander with the DFC & Bar.) An even more significant arrival came in the form of a new officer commanding on August 21: Wing Commander H M A Day.

Harry Melville Arbuthnot Day, who would later attain the soubriquet 'Wings' after the annual flying event, was a service man of the old school, although not originally in the RAF. Born in Sarawak, he had been educated in England at Haileybury, a school on the outskirts of Hertford that had originally been established to educate the boys of those serving with the East India Company. (Haileybury had a proud

'Wings' Day.

military tradition with the RFC and RAF. Old Haileyburians who distinguished themselves in the Second World War RAF include Sir John Slessor, Sir Trafford Leigh Mallory, and Sir William Dickson.)

Day volunteered for service in the Royal Marines in the First World War, serving on the battleship HMS *Britannia* and earning the nickname of 'the boy sprout' on the account of a sudden and unexpected growth spurt that took him above six feet. Two days before the armistice, HMS *Britannia* was torpedoed and began to sink. Day risked his own life by returning below decks through the smoke and the flames on two separate occasions to rescue two injured sailors – a feat for which he was afterwards awarded the Albert Medal (later to become the George Cross).

After the war he held a series of commands before transferring to the Fleet Air Arm and then the RAF as a flight lieutenant. He again came to the public's attention in the early 1930s when he was one of only a handful of skilled pilots to become part of a synchronised aerobatics display team that performed at Hendon and at other displays. His wingmen included a young and extremely self-confident pilot by the name of Douglas Bader, at that time still with his two legs attached.

Postings to RAF Abu Sueir and Khartoum were followed by promotion to squadron leader, ultimately returning to the UK to command the advanced flying training school at Little Rissington. Although comparatively old (he was by now forty), Day pestered his superiors for an active squadron command should war be declared, and with the war clouds looming, and now with the rank of wing commander, he was granted his wish.

Day, a strict disciplinarian, was not an instant hit with the men under his command:

> "On his first day in command he summoned us all on parade for an introduction. We were lined up in the hangar and I remember it was raining heavily outside. He said simply: 'All I want from my aircrew is for them to be smart. So get your hair cut, and make sure your boots are polished. Salute me first thing in the morning when you see me but after that just get on with your work.' That was our introduction to Wing Commander Day."

The previous OC, Wing Commander W L Payne, had been in charge since December 1936, and part of the problem was that the men had become used to him. They had formed crews that liked and respected one another, and flew well together. Day, however, had his own ideas and his own style. He seemed to be of the opinion that the squadron had become too flabby and comfortable, and that it needed a severe shake up to prepare them for what was to come. He had been in a war and so knew what to expect. One of his first actions, therefore, was to split up otherwise successful teams, as Alfie recalls:

> "I had grown to trust Johnnie as a pilot and very much resented being told I had to fly with another. The wing commander felt that things had become too cosy, and that all of the experience was concentrated into a small number of crews. By splitting us up he was trying to share the experience around, and so I found myself crewed with Flying Officer Mike Casey, although still with our regular gunner, 'Paddy' Nelson. Mike was a lovely man, and although not a patch on Johnnie as a pilot, he was at least lucky. Not long before I joined the squadron he had managed to crash land a Hawker Hind and end up with the aircraft on its nose and the tail sticking up in the air. He was lucky to walk away without breaking his neck."

Mike's luck may have had something to do with his Irish background. Born in Allahabad in 1918, his father was a senior official in the Indian Police. Mike was educated in England where he excelled at sport, impressing his peers with his mastery of the art of cricket and rugby, as well as showing true talent on the athletics track and in the boxing ring. His undoubted fighting spirit was balanced with a true devotion to his religion, taking his Catholic faith seriously at every stage of his life. Mike had joined the RAF in the summer of 1936, and was granted a short-service commission in a group of pilot officers that included Tom Kirby-Green, 'Pat' Pattle, Mike Beytagh and Roy Dutton★. By the time that he was paired with Alfie, he had risen to the rank of flying officer. His infectious energy and *bonhomie* made him one of the most popular characters on the squadron.

One of Alfie's first flights with Mike Casey almost proved to be their last. On the evening of August 8, they were detailed for a night flight to test a new piece of equipment – Identification Friend or Foe (IFF). IFF was a new technology that helped to differentiate between friendly and hostile aircraft by use of radar transmitters and receivers. One of the aircraft it was fitted to was Blenheim L1282. Alfie has good cause to remember that night well:

> "The number of trips we were flying in the summer and early autumn of 1939 increased considerably, as did the number of hours flown at night. On this particular evening we took off from Upper Heyford and set course for the Dutch coast. The idea was that we would stooge around the coastline for a short while and then after head home, giving our radar operators something to look at and to test our IFF.
>
> "We were up at about 9,000ft and all seemed well when suddenly it went pitch black, despite it being a beautiful summer's evening, and the aircraft went into a dive. To this day I do not know what happened, but I do know that all of the lights in the aircraft went out and a number of the flying instruments were smashed, making the Blenheim incredibly difficult to fly. We also lost a dramatic amount of height, the aircraft plummeting by some 7,000ft before Mike was able to regain some semblance of control.
>
> "Happily we were able to make the English coast at which point we started looking for somewhere to land. Looking beneath us I just managed to make out a cornfield that looked big enough and flat enough for us to make an emergency landing, and Mike began

---

★Kirby-Green was one of the fifty shot after the Great Escape; Marmaduke 'Pat' Pattle is widely considered to have been the top-scoring RAF ace of the war; while Mike Beytagh and Roy Dutton both distinguished themselves in the Battle of Britain and afterwards as fighter leaders.

bringing her down. It was only as we got closer, that I realised that at the end of the cornfield was a small copse, but by then it was too late and we were committed.

"We hit the ground hard at which point the aircraft again leaped into the air as if trying to take flight before bumping back down again with a mighty thud and a sickening scraping noise as the fuselage skidded and scraped across the field. Sitting in the nose was a terrifying sensation, and I remember Mike's hands were still on the control column as if he could steer the aircraft where he wanted, which of course he couldn't. Then we both saw the copse ahead of us and had that sickening sensation of knowing that we couldn't stop and we couldn't miss.

"But then we had our lucky break (I always said that Mike was a lucky pilot!). Miraculously, rather than hitting the trees we actually managed to go right through them, or at least the fuselage did. Both of the wings and the engines were torn off while me, Mike and the gunner continued sliding across the earth in what remained of the fuselage. It is the only time I have known an aircraft leave the ground with neither wings nor engines!"

Happily for Alfie and his compatriots, they managed to escape with a few minor bumps and bruises, and they were soon after returned to Upper Heyford to recount their experience.

Wing Commander Day took formal command of the squadron on August 21 and then immediately went on leave to share what would be the last holiday with his wife and children for almost six years. He was still on leave on August 23 when a postman tracked him down to the Norfolk Broads to deliver orders that the squadron would be mobilised, and he was to return forthwith. On the day of his return, Alfie had an opportunity to assess his new squadron commander's own flying abilities first hand:

"The wingco did not have his own crew and so flew whenever he could with whoever was available. He also didn't have much experience on Blenheims, and so wanted to increase his hours. The day after he returned from leave he grabbed me and another unsuspecting air gunner for a cross country, ostensibly, he said at the time, to test my own skills as a navigator. His wife, he told me, was holidaying in the Norfolk Broads, and my task was to find the yacht on which she and his family were cruising so that he could beat it up.

"There wasn't much preamble to the trip; we more or less just climbed in and took off, and soon we were skimming across the countryside towards Norfolk at little more than 500ft off the ground, with the countryside whizzing by, which made navigation difficult. Happily I found the Broads without too much bother and then we began a square search looking for her yacht. When we found it, the wingco buzzed the top of the yacht as close as he dared, and we could clearly see his wife and children waving back. After a couple of circuits, he told me to give him a course to steer for home.

"After we landed he said to me simply: 'Fripp, you were three minutes off your ETA [estimated time of arrival] and eight minutes getting home. Next time you will have to do better.' And at that, he marched away, leaving me somewhat dumbfounded. I may have not much liked his attitude, but there was no doubting his ability to fly an aeroplane."

The first order for the squadron to mobilise proved to be something of a false alarm and the order was rescinded, at least partially, the next day. It proved to be only a temporary respite, however, and over the course of the next few days the ground crews were kept busy preparing their aircraft for war. War markings were once again painted on the aircraft, this time for keeps. All leave was cancelled. Then on September 1, general mobilisation was ordered as news reached the British Cabinet that the Germans had attacked and invaded Poland. The squadron listened in silence and resignation to the announcement two days later that a state of war now existed with Germany.

The inevitability of war spurred Alfie into action in more ways than one. On the day that war was declared, he sought out the wing commander for permission to marry (he was not yet twenty-six and so formal permission was still required):

"We were at war but I was determined not to wait any longer to get married. I asked the CO for permission to marry and how much honeymoon I could have. He granted me a forty-eight-hour pass. I hurried down to Southampton in my motor car where my fiancé was living and rushed her back to Kidlington to stay with friends. I was obliged to fly a low-level trip to Bristol on the morning of

Alfie and Vera's wedding party, September 6 1939.

September 6, if I recall correctly, and returned shortly after midday,
just in time to get married that afternoon (at 2.00pm) at the
registry office in Carfax in the centre of Oxford. Johnnie Greenleaf
did the honours as best man. For 7/6 I got fifty-seven years of
happy married life!"

Mike Casey had similar thoughts. A friend of his at school had a sister, Margery.
Over time, Mike and Margery got to know each other until at last they too were
married at Bicester only days before the order was received to proceed to France.
The send off from the mess was described as a memorable affair, the bar only finally
being declared closed at five o'clock in the morning. After the shortest of short
honeymoons for both men they were soon back on the squadron, on their way to war.

CHAPTER THREE

————WAR PARTY————

Wing Commander Day received orders to take his squadron to Roye in France as part of an Expeditionary Force within the first few days of war being declared.

The British air forces in France were under the overall command of Air Marshal Arthur Barratt and divided into two subordinate formations: the RAF Component of the British Expeditionary Force commanded by Air Vice-Marshal Charles Blount whose actions would be dictated by the needs of the British Army, and the Advanced Air Striking Force (AASF) under the command of Air Vice-Marshal Patrick 'Pip' Playfair which would remain part of Bomber Command. ★

Day and his squadron would be part of the Air Component, alongside 53 Squadron – another Blenheim strategic-reconnaissance unit – four Lysander squadrons (for tactical reconnaissance), and two fighter squadrons flying the Hawker Hurricane. Two further Blenheim units – 18 and 59 Squadrons – had both a dual reconnaissance and bombing role.

———

*Barratt later became Air Chief Marshal Sir Arthur Barratt KCB, CMG, MC. He acquired the somewhat unfair nickname of 'Ugly'; Blount was killed in an air accident in October 1940 three days short of his forty-seventh birthday; Playfair later became Air Marshal Sir Patrick Playfair KBE, CB, CVO, MC.

It was a strange and slightly anti-climactic time for Alfie and his colleagues. The immediate air raids that had been expected from the all-conquering Luftwaffe failed to materialise, and it was as though neither side wanted to engage in full-on military conflict too early, or make the first move. The frailties of the opposing factions had not yet been exposed although they would shortly, with disturbing and illusion-shattering consequences for the RAF.

Even though it had been planned for some time, there were, of course, a number of practical issues with moving military units overseas and 57 Squadron had more issues than most. Being a reconnaissance unit it had more personnel and equipment than 'normal' Blenheim squadrons and was almost entirely self-contained with its own cooks, kitchens and petrol supplies should it be obliged to move bases at short notice. The advance party left for Southampton on September 12, followed four days later by the transport component; the main party did not leave until six days later, taking the train from Bicester to the docks and setting sail later that afternoon. The party eventually disembarked at Cherbourg and entrained for Roye.

The ground parties were somewhat dismayed by what they found at Roye and the neighbouring airfield at Amy, a village four miles to the south where they would be billeted. They say that an army marches on its stomach, and it is clear from the entry in the squadron's ORB for September 24 that food was very much on the minds of the airmen too:

> 'Rations supplied and cooked by French troops guarding the aerodrome. The rations comprise of: breakfast – bread and coffee; lunch – meat soup, vegetable, bread and wine; and supper – as for lunch. The airmen did not complain of the quantity or quality but of the method of cooking.'

The abundance of wine, at least, helped counteract some of their frustrations. Keeping clean was also a challenge for there were no baths and only limited washing facilities. The ORB also tells of the haphazard billeting affair and conditions: 'The officers and NCOs were billeted in houses in the village; the airmen in the farms. Straw used as bedding.'

The pilots and aircrew did not fly out from Upper Heyford until September 30, by which time the main transport had arrived in Amy and the troops were being sustained by solid British cooking which did wonders for morale. Bell tents surrounded the grass airfield that was by now a hive of activity. But while the food was improving, and the transport and equipment had arrived, the conditions were still far from satisfactory for housing an entire squadron. Flight Lieutenant Geoff Wyatt, a contemporary of Alfie's at that time, described the accommodation as being 'rough to the point of squalor', and he was an officer. The airmen had it much worse.

Wyatt remembered one large billet in the loft of some stables, and the coincidence of one corporal reservist, with a *Croix de Guerre* from the First World War, who had been billeted in exactly the same spot during the earlier contest!

Notwithstanding the conditions, and in the true British tradition of 'making do', the squadron soon found its own routine, helped by the officer commanding who ordered a daily morning parade of the whole squadron to keep them apprised of developments and to allocate training and various other duties. Not that there was a great deal to report. An address was also given by the air officer commanding (AOC) Air Component, Air-Vice Marshal Charles Blount OBE, MC. Blount had learned to fly in 1916 and later went on to command a squadron of RE8 bomber/ reconnaissance aircraft. He knew what was expected of him and reminded the men of the essential role that they were about to play as the eyes and ears of the ground troops, and that they would shortly be embarking on a series of long-range reconnaissance flights (referred to as 'Strat.Rs') into Germany.

The squadron had yet to be called upon for assistance, but perhaps in that respect it had been lucky. The first foray by a Blenheim squadron into Germany had been an absolute disaster when four of their number had been shot down attacking shipping in Wilhelmshaven – and they had been flying the faster and more-advanced Blenheim IV. In France, two Fairey Battles of 88 Squadron had been shot down while on reconnaissance and four airmen killed. There had been much hope for the Fairey Battle, an aircraft that had been a revolutionary design in its day as a single-engine monoplane bomber, but that day had already passed. Two days before 57 Squadron's aircraft arrived in France, two more Blenheim IVs had been shot down on reconnaissance, both from 110 Squadron. All six aircrew perished, including the officer commanding, Wing Commander I Cameron, who was shot down near Münster. The portents were far from encouraging.

But the biggest disaster occurred on the same day that the first of 57 Squadron's Blenheims touched down at Amy, when no fewer than five Battles from 150 Squadron were lost to German fighters in the space of an hour. It was proof, if further was needed, of the woeful inadequacy of the RAF's front-line bomber and reconnaissance aircraft of the time, although far greater tragedies would unfold later. But by then, Alfie's war was already over.

Wing Commander Day agitated for operations until at last he was summoned to wing headquarters at the Renaissance chateau of Tilloloy and told that two aircraft were to be on constant standby, lest they were needed at short notice. A forward air base was established at Metz, closer to the border with Germany, and from where any operations would be flown. An alternative advanced-landing ground was also established at Étain, just in case the first was put out of service.

On October 8, two aircraft flew to Metz in preparation for operations that were soon after cancelled because of bad weather. They returned on the 10th. On the afternoon of October 12, six aircraft – one flown by the wing commander – flew down to Metz and awaited further instruction. At last it came. Two aircraft were to conduct long-range reconnaissance sorties into Germany, the first to do a reconnaissance of the roads and railways in the areas of Hamm, Hannover and Soest, and the second to reconnoitre the railways between Münster and Bremen. Perhaps not surprisingly, the wing commander volunteered to fly the squadron's first operation himself, determined to lead from the front and not ask other men to do something he was not prepared to do himself. He would take with him his young navigator, Sergeant Eric Hillier, and Leading Aircraftman Frederick Moller as his wireless op/air gunner. The second crew he selected from 'B' Flight comprised Flying Officer Clive Norman, Sergeant Edwards and Aircraftman Jervis as pilot, navigator and w/op air gunner respectively. Alfie remembers:

> "Before setting off, at one of our morning parades the CO told us that he thought we were all getting a little jittery. The war was now several weeks old but not a great deal had happened. Although we had flown a number of training flights, I think all of us were anxious to get started. The wing commander seemed to sense this and told us he would be flying the first sortie himself. There was no precedent for it. His intention, however, was clear. He wanted to show us that there was nothing to be afraid of. I also think he wanted to see for himself what operations were like, so that he could impart his knowledge onto us. He didn't need to do it, and I don't remember being especially impressed, but you couldn't fault his enthusiasm."

Day took off from Metz at 11.40. The weather was perfect, indeed a little too perfect for it left the wing commander with nowhere to hide should they be seen and intercepted by German fighters. Climbing through broken cloud, Day took the Blenheim to 22,000ft, somewhat short of its theoretical maximum ceiling. Above cloud now he took stock. He knew that above cloud he was comparatively safe. He also knew that he would need to dip below it in order to photograph anything of interest. He regretted not being more forceful with his superiors about the need for a fighter escort, or to wait until the weather conditions were more favourable. He regretted also not having the newer mark of Blenheim that was then coming in to service – the Mk IV – with its superior performance. A Mk IV was faster and more powerful than its predecessor, with far greater endurance and range. When he was perhaps fifty or so miles inside of German airspace, his mind was made up for him. The cloud disappeared, leaving him in a clear sky in brilliant sunshine, and in very great danger.

The Met forecast had promised cloud cover all over Germany. Not for the first time, the weather men were wrong, and no doubt he would have a thing or two to say about that when he got home. But for now he had other things to worry about, and his concerns grew greater still when his gunner began reporting the first signs of flak – dirty little puffs of black smoke telling him that they had been seen. The wing commander held his height and course while the navigator peered below to identify their position. More flak began appearing and then an even greater menace: fighters.

The flak was being used to steer the fighters onto the target, a tactic that was as old as the hills. Very soon there were three of the Luftwaffe's best fighters, the Messerschmitt Bf109, heading towards the Blenheim in line astern. Until then, Day had only seen such fighters in the pages of *The Aeroplane* or *Flight* magazines, or as silhouettes to aid aircraft recognition. He knew they meant trouble. Instinctively, Day turned the aircraft to face the attack, hoping perhaps to make use of the single fixed .303 Browning machine gun mounted in the port wing. As he did so he heard and felt the first machine-gun and canon shells thumping into the fuselage and wings of his aircraft. Pushing the throttles 'through the gate' to give him maximum boost, the engines screamed as he twisted and turned the Blenheim as best he could to avoid their attacks. Then everything seemed to happen in a flash. Small wisps of smoke began filling the cockpit and then the self-sealing fuel tanks were set on fire and the wisps turned to clouds of smoke that fully obscured his vision. He could now no longer see his hands in front of him nor have any recollection as regards whether his fellow crewmates were still onboard, or whether they had baled out.[*]

Reaching above him he grasped for the escape hatch and hauled himself up, terrified that he might hit the tailplane as his sizeable frame was almost sucked out of the cockpit. Then the aircraft fell apart. As he tumbled through the air he felt for the cold metal of the parachute's D-ring, removing his gloves to find it and desperately trying to remember the drill. Just then he saw a Bf109 flash by, and with no wish to become the first RAF airman in the Second World War to be shot whilst dangling from his 'chute, delayed pulling the D-ring until he was convinced he was out of danger. Happily the parachute above him opened with a loud 'crack', and as he floated to earth he had the disconcerting sensation of seeing and sensing parts of his burning aircraft falling close by.

At Metz, however, they had no idea of the drama that was unfolding. An hour

---

[*]Day's victor is reported as being Oberfeldwebel Ernst Vollmer (4/JG53). Vollmer himself was shot down and killed in the summer of 1940.

57 Squadron at Rosières, October 1939.

after the CO's take-off, Flying Officer Norman had left to reconnoitre the railways between Münster and Bremen, and report any significant troop movements. He had rather better luck than his CO, encountering some flak but avoiding any fighter interference, and eventually making it back to England. Short of fuel, and with the weather closing in, Norman crash-landed and escaped with his crew unhurt.

As the afternoon turned to evening, it became clear that the CO would not be coming back:

> "Nobody seemed particularly alarmed that the wing commander was gone. You would have thought that losing your commanding officer on our first operation of the war would have had some impact, but I don't recall any real emotion. It was all a bit surreal, and I think we thought that he was bound to turn up sooner or later. The concept that he was missing was easy enough to accept, but we never for a moment thought that he or any of his crew might be dead."

As it was, Wing Commander Day had had a somewhat miraculous escape. Friday 13th had proved to be lucky for one. But it was not such a lucky day for his two crewmen. Just as Day had baled out, the Blenheim had exploded. Eye-witnesses reported seeing three men escaping from the aircraft, but two of these men were on fire. Eric Hillier and Frederick Moller did not survive and thus became the squadron's first casualties of the war. Squadron Leader Arthur Garland assumed command of the squadron.

On October 16, a further reconnaissance flight was ordered for the 'Southern

Route' (the flight taken by Day had been known as the 'Northern Route') to report on movement along the railway line between Wesel and Bocholt, north west of Essen in the Ruhr. As mentioned earlier, the crew detailed for operations was Flying Officer Mike Casey (pilot); Sergeant Alfie Fripp (observer); and Aircraftman 'Paddy' Nelson (wireless op/air gunner). The aircraft was Blenheim L1141:

> "On the morning of October 16 we were told that it was us who would be making the next trip. I didn't feel nervous or apprehensive or anything, but rather excited. This was what we had trained to do and now we were doing it. We flew first to the alternative advanced-landing ground at Étain, a short hop, and refuelled. By 11.00hrs we were ready, and after a quick if somewhat bumpy take-off on a grass strip, I gave Mike the course to steer to undertake the first part of our photo reconnaissance.
>
> "We had been told that we were to receive a Hurricane escort, but for whatever reason the fighter boys didn't turn up and we were left to our own devices. Perhaps their aircraft were u/s or perhaps they were needed elsewhere. I never did find out. We knew that it would be dangerous, but we were still confident that we would make it back in one piece. A little way into our operation and the flak started to fly about. It looked harmless enough but we knew what it meant. It meant that there was a good chance there could be fighters about, so we decided to get a move on.
>
> "Cloud base over the target was about 10,000ft so we descended below it. I clambered into the back to the bomb well to set the F8 camera running and thought that we got a good line overlap of the railways lines and various troop concentrations. Then Mike started looking for some cloud cover to keep us hidden. Before he was able to find any, however, Paddy reported that he could see an enemy fighter closing in on us, and then all hell let loose."

What happened next was detailed in a contemporary newspaper report in Germany. At that time, the shooting down of a British aircraft was worthy of significant press interest, and the reporter who interviewed the victorious German pilot for the *Westfälische Landeszeitung* was eloquent with his description:

> 'I was sitting in my machine somewhere in Ems at ten minutes past three last Tuesday afternoon when an enemy scout was reported flying from the north at a height of little more than 100ft. When the Englishman [sic], whom I could plainly see in his machine, was

flying over us I took off. Anti-aircraft artillery came into action, and to avoid this I rose to some height. The enemy swung round to westward, seeking a cloud in which to escape. He swerved sharply, lessening considerably my chances of hitting him. I followed close at his heels and, seeing that he could not shake me off, he went into a spin dive into a cloudbank about 200 metres in depth. I dived even more steeply. As I came out of the cloudbank, I saw him emerge from the cloud above me.

'He again dived and then there was a mad pursuit which almost beggars description. The Englishman was an adroit and skillful airman. He utilised every unevenness in the ground, every hedge, every ditch as cover. He slipped between trees and skimmed over houses. As I raced on I could see the smashed tree tops against the sky and the broken bushes flying through the air. Now and again I expected to see him remove a roof but with his speed of 300 kilometres an hour he jumped over every obstacle. At times we were barely six feet from the ground, and even eye-witnesses thought he was down. But he went on, although escape now was out of the question.

'At last after another volley I saw the pilot lay his machine on the ground and three occupants jumped out. They had not had time to release the landing gear of the aeroplane which was already in flames; and it simply crashed into a potato field. I circled above them and they greeted me with clasped hands, as if to say that they would like to shake hands with me after a chivalrous fight.'*

The words of the victor – identified in the report simply as 'Leutnant K'*– differ somewhat from the words of the vanquished, albeit that the outcome was the same.

---

*It should be noted that translations and interpretations of the event vary. Alfie remembers giving the pilot a two-fingered salute!

*'Leutnant K' as reported in the English newspapers was in fact Leutnant 'R' – the old German letter script having been misinterpreted. Leutnant 'R' was subsequently identified as Leutnant Hans-Folkert Rosenboom of 3/JG1 and the Blenheim was his first 'kill'. Rosenboom would go on to shoot down two French bombers and a further RAF Blenheim the following spring, before losing his life in a collision with his wingman near the Isle of Wight on August 16, 1940. His wingman, Unteroffizier Erich Ackmann, survived, only to be shot down and killed ten days later.

Alfie remembers:

> "The enemy's first burst smashed through the rear fuselage, just missing Paddy but knocking out his gun and rendering us defenceless. It sounded like a tin of rusty nails being shaken about as the shells hit us. Now there was only Mike and his flying skills to rely upon to get us out of danger. And Mike put on a virtuoso performance. Recognising that our only chance of escape was to dive for the deck, he did exactly that, taking the Blenheim to almost zero feet and zooming along the ground. It was both exhilarating and terrifying in equal measure, and I had the grandstand seat."

The Blenheim roared over the German countryside, the engines screaming in complaint at the incredible strain Mike was putting them under, throttles fully forward:

> "We had an indicated airspeed of more than 200mph, which when you are only a handful of feet off the ground and can see trees and rooftops so close to you that you feel you can reach out and touch them, seems even faster. I had little thought about navigation at this point, other than we wanted to make for Holland, and anyway it would have been virtually impossible to navigate with any accuracy at that height."

Casey jinked the Blenheim from side to side and bobbed and weaved like a boxer trying to avoid the knockout blow, for that was precisely what they were doing. They were in a mad steeplechase and Mike was using every tree, hill and house as cover. The lucky rabbit foot he always carried with him seemed to be holding good.

They tore between trees, whipping off branches and seeing hedges and haystacks flattened in their wake. As the Blenheim danced, so too the German fighter pilot kept pace, occasionally firing off the odd burst to let them know he was still right behind them. Every time they approached an obstacle, it seemed that they must be doomed, but somehow Mike avoided them all. It seemed for a few fleeting moments that they might still get away with it but then finally, inevitably perhaps, their luck ran out:

> "One of the German's bursts of cannon and machine-gun fire hit something vital, and smoke began filling the cockpit. A pair of engine covers that had been stowed in the bomb bay began smoldering and the smell soon reached my nostrils. Then Mike

at last misjudged his height and we struck a tree, shattering our windscreen and so too our hopes of reaching friendly territory. The port engine gave out and Mike had no choice but to crash land.

"With our wheels up, and the one remaining good engine shut down, Mike said: 'I'm sorry – here we go,' and eased the aircraft onto the ground in a near-perfect wheels-up belly landing, the Blenheim sliding evenly across a field full of potatoes. The noise was incredible as we cut a swathe through the comparatively-soft earth, but this was the second time in as many months that we had crash-landed and I knew what to expect. The aircraft at last came to a halt as it dug its nose into the earth, and there was a second's pause as we thanked God that we were alive.

"Then we smelled the fire; the petrol had escaped from the broken fuel lines and made contact with the hot engines, with the inevitable result. In double-quick time we released the escape hatch and climbed out of the now-burning aircraft. Very cartridges began exploding and with the fire it looked for all the world like bonfire night. Save for a few cuts and bruises, we were all otherwise in one piece and the relief was palpable. The gravity of our situation was not yet apparent; for the moment, we were airmen who had simply got away with a dodgy landing. Still perhaps in shock, we saw a farmer bounding across the field, shotgun in hand and gesticulating wildly."

The aircraft came down at Fürstenau, just north west of Osnabrück, at 15.30 local time. They were only a few minutes flying time from neutral Holland and safety.

CHAPTER FOUR
━━━━━━━━━IN THE BAG━━━━━━━━━

The Blenheim had a maximum endurance just short of six hours, depending on how kind the pilot was with the throttles. By the early evening the new squadron commander, Arthur Garland, resigned himself to the loss of another crew. There was a chance, of course, that they had made it back to England, and good news might still follow. Alternatively they may have been obliged to put down somewhere in neutral territory and been interned. It was not unheard of. Later there would be a wonderful story recounted in fighter circles of the 'Prisoner of Luxembourg', a pilot shot down and interned after a forced landing at an airfield in the Grand Duchy, and who would later return to his squadron. All they could do for the time being was to write up the squadron ORB with the simple words: 'Did not return.' The crew was also officially posted as 'missing'.

Squadron life, however, continued. The very next day, Flight Lieutenant Geoffrey Wyatt and his crew comprising Sergeant 'Rocky' Gardner and LAC 'Jack' Russell had more luck with their reconnaissance foray into Germany. They too were initially protected by cloud, but this soon gave way to reveal 'a hell of a lot of Germany ahead in a beautiful, cloudless autumn day'.* With only a general idea of

━━━━━━━━

*(Norman Franks – *Valiant Wings*).

their location, they proceeded to photograph anything and everything in the hope that they might capture something of interest until they arrived over Bremen and had their first experience of flak. Discretion being the better part of valour, Wyatt did not stay long over the German port and opted to head home to the UK over the North Sea, keeping a watchful look out for enemy fighters all the way. They landed, exhausted, at Honington, and thence on to Upper Heyford and a well-earned 'beat up' of a local hostelry.

But while Wyatt and his friends were celebrating, Alfie and his crew were experiencing their first taste of German captivity. Airmen of 1939 were ill-prepared for wartime operations and certainly ill-prepared for escape. Later – much later – with the establishment of MI9, a dedicated service set up specifically to support escape and evasion, the chances of escape were improved, and the quality of intelligence, equipment and training given to aircrew greatly enhanced. Those who succeeded in getting away, and making it home, had much vital knowledge and experience to impart. But for now they had nothing. The civilian education officer on the squadron had been taken on as the intelligence officer when the squadron moved to France and the sum total of his experience was zero. The issue of what to do if shot down was hardly mentioned, and if it wasn't discussed then it could never happen. Escape kits, compasses and maps that would become *de rigeur* for future aircrew had not even been considered. Indeed the crew had received no advice or briefing beyond that if they were to be captured by the Germans they were to reveal only their name, rank and number!

After being accosted by the farmer and his shotgun, a party of German soldiers quickly arrived having watched the Blenheim come down. The funeral pyre of Alfie's aircraft served as a beacon for virtually every German unit in the area. Herded onto an army truck and with the familiar phrase 'for you the war is over' still ringing in their ears, the three men sat with their German guards and contemplated their fate. The best chance of escape was always within the first few hours when it was least expected but the three men were still somewhat traumatised by their ordeal. Escape was not on their minds – at least not for the time being. That time would come.

The truck took them to Münster, where they were imprisoned at the local air headquarters. They were immediately separated and escorted to individual rooms – probably NCO's quarters – where they would wait until their interrogation would begin. This was a testing time for any man, however brave, and especially for those in shock. Together, they could derive courage from one another. But separated, alone with one's thoughts and one's fears, the mind could be inclined to become somewhat overactive, and it was the consequences of what might happen that began to gnarl at the nerves.

Soon it became Alfie's turn for interrogation, and he was collected from his room and taken to the interrogator's office. The interview did not last long: Alfie stood resolutely to instructions, and gave nothing but his name, rank and number. He was then handed a form that purported to be from the Red Cross, and was asked to fill it in. He was told that it was needed so that his next of kin could be notified that he was alive and well. Beyond name, rank and number, however, the form included questions of a more precise military nature and Alfie refused to answer.

The scene was repeated the next day and the next, although the duration of the interviews became longer, and the interrogator's questions more demanding: What was the strength of the Royal Air Force in France? Where were the units located? What reinforcements could the air force expect to receive from England? How many British troops were in France? How did we communicate with our French allies and what connections did we have with them on the Maginot Line? Alfie continued to prevaricate, repeating his name, rank and number, and comfortable with the thought that as a mere sergeant, most of the questions being asked of him he couldn't possibly know the answer to anyway:

> "After three days of just giving my name, rank and number it was clear that the Germans were getting a little fed up with me. Then they surprised me by saying: 'don't worry if you do not answer. We know all of the answers already from your Wing Commander Day.' I did not think for a moment that Day had told them anything and it was just a bluff to get me talking, but it was reassuring nonetheless that our commanding officer was alive, for that was the first news we had received of his fate."

Much has been written about chivalry in the air in both world wars. There was certainly a precedent – in the early days at least – for victorious fighter pilots to 'honour' their vanquished foe, if and when duty allowed. And so it was that on the last night of their stay in Münster, Alfie, Mike and Paddy were invited to the officers' mess of JagdGeschwader 1 (JE1) to dine as guests of honour. Although allowed time to wash and shave, the RAF men still looked somewhat outclassed in appearance against the magnificent blue uniforms of their Luftwaffe counterparts, and the pretty dresses of their ladies:

> "It was the first opportunity we'd had to be together for some time and that was a relief. There was plenty to eat and drink and Mike said that whatever we do, we must not drink too much. In fact,

he said that it was better if we didn't drink at all. The Germans had brought their girlfriends along with them, many of whom could speak English. It quickly became clear by the nature of their questioning that they had been given instructions to find out as much as they could about us, but we knew what they were up to and said nothing.

"Towards the end of the evening, their commanding officer stood up to say a few words and make a toast. In halting English he praised all brave airmen and said that his men were heroes. Mike didn't like this and stood up to interrupt him, which caused quite a stir. 'Sir,' he said. 'The real heroes in this war will be the women and the children.' At that, the evening seemed to come to an abrupt end and we were not allowed to finish our dinner. The guard was called and quickly afterwards we once again heard the room door clanging shut behind us."

The next morning the three men were roused early and again pushed and prodded into the back of a wagon for a destination unknown. The mystery deepened as they were taken to the local railway station to suffer the bemused stares of their fellow travellers as though exhibits in some bizarre museum of curiosities. In time, the German civilians would come to loathe and despise the RAF bomber crews, even so far as to calling them gangsters and *'Terror Fliegers'* (terror flyers). Occasionally, crews would be openly assaulted in public, and even had to look to their German guards for protection. Later still, some would be murdered. But for now they were safe.

Their journey took them to the village of Spangenberg and Mike Casey was escorted from the train. Paddy and Alfie remained seated until their next and final destination, Moosburg, on the outskirts of Munich.

———————

While Alfie was enduring his first few days of captivity, in England his wife Vera had been in a constant state of anxiety since receiving the dreaded telegram to say that he was 'missing'. It was such a small and yet terribly disconsolate word that could mean everything or it could mean nothing. Missing could simply be that with no news, there was nothing left to be said. Or it could mean that he had literally 'disappeared', as had so many in the first war with no known grave. She was understandably distraught that her husband of only a handful of weeks had been so cruelly and unfairly taken from her, and now she hoped and prayed that she would soon receive news that he was safe and well, and perhaps even now on his way home or back to his squadron.

Then on October 20 she received the news she had been hoping for. The first indication that Alfie was alive:

> 'Unconfirmed report by German pilot states your son 565033 Fripp landed by parachute on German territory. Taken Prisoner. Confirmation will be forwarded when received.'

The report was at fault in its minor detail. Alfie had not, of course, escaped by parachute, but the main tenet of the message was still accurate: he was a prisoner of war. Four days later, Alfie's parents received a short letter from a Squadron Leader Saunders on behalf of the AOC in charge of RAF records. It read:

> 'The Allied Press Agency are in possession of unconfirmed information. A German pilot reports that Flying Officer M J Casey, Sergeant A G Fripp, and Aircraftman 2nd Class J Nelson have landed by parachute in Germany and are consequently Prisoners of War. Directly we have confirmation of this we will communicate with you.'

The report again seemed to suggest that Alfie had baled out, but again it appeared to confirm he was safe, and mentioned that his two crewmates were also safe. Squadron Leader Garland, the OC 57 Squadron, wrote to Vera on October 26:

> 'It was a great relief to us the other day to hear the very good news that your husband has been reported as being a prisoner of war after having been missing for several days. We were full of admiration for him and the remainder of the crew when we heard the wonderful account they had given of themselves against heavy enemy opposition and you must well be proud of him, as also we are. On behalf of myself and all other ranks in the squadron, I wish to extend to you our deep regret that he will be separated both from you and us for the remainder of the war, but we must earnestly trust that its conclusion will see his safe return in good health and spirits.'

The Germans had expected to take prisoners, but in the first stages of the war in the west there appeared to be little or no provision for RAF prisoners of war specifically. Indeed no Luftwaffe-run permanent POW camp would exist until the middle of

1940 and as such, RAF officers and men found themselves in all manner of camps and moving around with disturbing regularity.

Moosburg, Alfie's first Kriegie (short for *Kriegsgefangener* – literally 'war prisoner') home was in fact a Wehrmacht camp, administered by the German army for army prisoners of war. Officially designated Stalag VII A (the name Stalag is an abbreviation of *Stammlager* or 'base camp') and located less than a mile from the town itself, Moosburg lay in rolling, hilly countryside on the west bank of the River Isar. The camp was not much to look at beyond a large open space, with an enormous perimeter swept by searchlights and machine guns housed in some six guard towers. The huts and barracks, such as they were, were contained within two wire fences that were themselves in-filled with concertina wire. The Kommandant was a German officer of the old school, Oberst Hans Nepf.

Alfie and Paddy were eyed with deep suspicion by the existing inmates – a mixture of French and Poles captured during some of the early fighting. They were already well settled, and disinclined to share their amenities:

> "We were given a tent, some straw and a single blanket and had to make the best of it. We made a scraping in the ground and by pulling the blanket over us and the straw on top, we were able to keep warm enough although it could be bitterly cold. For food we were given a baked potato each by some of the Poles, and that was our first real introduction to how scarce food was to become, and yet how important it would be to our lives and survival."

The reality of being no longer in charge of their own destinies was brought home the following day when they were again paraded for their heads to be shaved. The official reason given was to control lice but there was no doubt that the Germans enjoyed the air of superiority that it gave them in humiliating their charges. This, Alfie says, was part of the initiation into prisoner life:

> "Of course we objected strongly and there was an altercation with the guards but it was of no use. We felt that we were still airmen, not common criminals, and should not be treated as criminals. The Germans had other ideas, and after a few well-aimed rifle butts in the ribs and on our backs we were obliged to do as we were told. After our heads were shaved we were then led into the showers. We learned then that it was better not to protest."

The boredom of those first few weeks was punctuated by the occasional visit by youngsters from the nearby town, all of whom were members of the local

Alfie with his head shaved, Moosburg, October 1939.

Reichsarbeitsdienst (RAD) and national socialists to the core. They were intrigued by the two RAF men and indeed not unfriendly. They would strike up conversations to practice their English and toss the occasional hunk of bread over the fence to supplement the airmen's meagre diet. The friendly relations did not continue for long, however. On November 8, an apprentice cabinetmaker planted a bomb in a Munich *Bierkeller* with the intention of killing the Führer. The bomb exploded, killing eight people and wounding sixty-five others, but Adolf Hitler escaped unscathed. It was enough to taint all of those who opposed Germany, and so the fraternisation quickly ended:

"The Germans were very organised in every respect other than food. Sometimes we had nothing more than a hunk of black bread and a little margarine to last us through the day. To drink we were given 'coffee'. It was not real coffee but rather what they called 'Ersatz' (imitation) coffee that was made using burned acorns. The taste was terrible to start off with but you got used to it over time."

It was while he was at Moosburg that Alfie's family finally found out for certain that he was alive when a letter reached Vera – a letter in Alfie's distinctive hand. As a contemporary newspaper report at the time suggested, it made her 'the happiest woman in Wimborne'. The words were carefully chosen, with humour and reassurance, and suggested nothing of the trauma her husband had recently gone through:

'Don't worry because I shall soon be back with you once again. Germany is a nice country. I think we will come here on our honeymoon.

'We were shot down by the German fighter boys and, believe me, all three of us stepped out of the 'plane with only a few scratches and bruises. We are all prisoners of war, and for us there will be no more fighting. We have travelled much of Germany since we came down on October 16 and have finished up here (at Oberbayern). Everywhere we have been has seen us enjoying the hospitality of the German people. Nobody in Germany wants war, just the same as in England.

'Our quarters here are very good, and we are in here with three Frenchmen. All we need is a Folies Bergere chorus to walk in to make a party. We are like a band of comrades and, in fact, a happy band of pilgrims.

A week later and there was more reassuring news when Alfie's voice was heard on the radio. The Germans were quick to recognise the importance of propaganda and used it to maximum effect throughout the war. From the outset they had used Alfie's crash and the experiences of other downed and captured airmen as an opportunity to promote the superiority of the Luftwaffe over the RAF; now they wished to go a step further and offered Alfie and a number of fellow prisoners the opportunity of broadcasting a message home to their respective families:

"When we were first taken to Moosburg we knew that there was no way of letting our people know at home that we were safe. We knew that they would worry we were dead. We discussed it between us and decided that if there were ever an opportunity to get a message out, we would take it.

"The Germans approached us one day and asked whether we would like to broadcast a message home. I knew we were being used but the Germans held us to ransom. They said that if we did not do as they instructed, then they would not contact the Red Cross, and any help that we might receive would not be given. On reflection perhaps we should have refused, but at the time it seemed like the right decision."

Whatever the moral rights or wrongs, Alfie's broadcast had the desired effect. Seven men★ were brought to the microphone to record a series of messages for the Berlin radio station DJN (broadcast on the German short-wave 19 metre band). After a short description of life in a prisoner-of-war camp – a camp where there was said to be around 4,000 Poles and 400 French Poilus – the men sent their best wishes in the hope that someone at home would hear them. Happily there were a sufficient number of radio 'hams' listening in to have the impact they desired. Alfie remembers:

"I was the first to speak and remember sending my best wishes to Vera and telling her that I was very well and she was not to worry. I hoped very much that she would enjoy Christmas as much as if I were there with her. I couldn't be sure that anyone would hear us, but I gave my address (340 Burgess Road) and said that my parents came from Wimborne and if anyone knew them or my wife to let them know."

★The other men identified in the broadcast included Aircraftman Pacey of Redford, Nottinghamshire and Sergeant Springett of Radlett, Hertfordshire. Aircraftman Pacey had been taken prisoner on September 9, having been shot down on a Nickel operation over the Ruhr. Pacey, and his 102 Squadron crew, had the distinction of becoming the first complete bomber crew to be taken into captivity; Sergeant Springett had been shot down on September 30 undertaking an early reconnaissance in a Fairy Battle of 150 Squadron. Both his pilot and air gunner were killed. The other men identified in the local newspaper report at the time were: 'Sergeant Lambeth' and 'Aircraftman Berrett', both of Oldfield; 'Private Dunton' of Northumberland; and 'Sergeant Shuttleworth'.

It is possible that the name of 'Lambeth' was in fact Sergeant J W Lambert, shot down as part of a 77 Squadron crew lost on the night of October 15/16.

Vera did not hear the broadcast personally, but the good news was not slow in being reported. She was, understandably, overcome with joy. And it seems that her joy was shared by the whole nation, for two days later she received no fewer than three sacks full of letters from well-wishers who had heard the broadcast.

There was perhaps even greater joy, if such things can truly be measured, for the parents of Paddy Nelson in Belfast. Paddy, it transpired, had been first reported missing and soon after reported dead. Nelson, in his broadcast, asked that anyone who happened to hear him should communicate with his father and mother and his friend Kenneth Murdoch and say that he was well.

Alfie and Paddy's time at Moosburg was shortlived. One morning they were told to pack what little belongings and personal kit they had accumulated for they were once again on the move, this time to be reunited albeit briefly with their skipper and commanding officer.

Spangenberg was in fact a camp intended for officers and was officially Offizierslager (Oflag) IXA. It was located some twenty-five kilometres south east of Kassel, and like its much more famous counterpart – Colditz – the camp comprised a 13th Century *Schloss* high on a hill overlooking the villages of Spangenberg and Elbersdorf, and surrounded by woodland.

The castle dominated the area with its 100ft high, grey-stone walls and imposing clock tower and turrets that encased an inner courtyard. The dramatic scene was further brought into focus by the deep moat and drawbridge, across which all prisoners would be led, avoiding the three wild boar that appeared to roam freely about. The castle was no stranger to prisoners. It had held French prisoners in 1870 during the Franco-Prussian war, and French and British prisoners during the First World War. It was not a surprise, therefore, that its services had been called upon once again. It was not a surprise, also, to hear that as yet, no-one had ever escaped.

———————

It was a depressing and intimidating sight as the two airmen entered through the gate for the first time, only to find themselves coming face to face with a familiar figure:

> "As they opened the gate, the first person I could see walking around was our commanding officer, Wing Commander Day. He looked at me and nodded, adding rather casually: 'Ah, good morning Fripp', to which I replied 'good morning sir', and that was it. It was as though we were still at home on the station, and not hundreds of miles away locked up in a prisoner-of-war camp in Germany."

The incident is remembered in Wings Day's biography, written by Sydney Smith in 1968. Smith wrote:

> 'The sight of young Fripp coming in across the drawbridge, bearded, scruffy, was a link with those magic days of peace, and that last glimpse of excited little figures waving a farewell for longer than they had dreamed.'

Alfie was quickly to discover other familiar faces from 57 Squadron: as well as the CO, there was also his own pilot, Mike Casey, looking a little leaner but otherwise fit and well, and another of the officers, 'Pop' Bewlay with his trademark pipe still clenched firmly between his teeth. Bewlay, Alfie learned, had been shot down only a short while after their own adventure. Indeed, three weeks after Alfie's loss, Pilot Officer Alexander Morton and his crew had all been lost on another wasteful reconnaissance of the Siegfried Line. The very next day, November 7, 'Pop' and his crew had taken off on a similar sortie and got as far as Mainz before they fell foul of a combination of poor weather and the attentions of Joachim Müncheberg of JG26*, and were shot down for Müncheberg's first victory of the war. It did not make cheerful listening, and what they did not know was that things would get worse. By the end of 1939 and what the people at home were calling 'The Phoney War' as nothing seemed to be happening, almost half of the squadron had been lost before finally someone had realised that sending unescorted Blenheims on long-range sorties over Germany in daylight was tantamount to suicide. There was nothing 'phoney' about telegrams being sent to loved ones to tell them that their sons or husbands might not be coming back.

Accommodation at Spangenberg was spartan at best, but at least it was a considerable improvement from sleeping in tents out in the open air, and Alfie had an iron bedstead as opposed to a scraping in the ground. The beds were in long rows in a communal barrack room on the ground floor. They were lucky; previous

---

*Bewlay makes no mention of being shot down, but rather falling victim to ice. Müncheberg went on to shoot down a total of 135 aircraft before being killed in action in the Western Desert in 1943.

prisoners had been obliged to sleep in the cellar. In the middle of the room were two long tables with wooden benches on either side. It was at these tables that the prisoners would sit, eat and compare experiences.

There was much to contemplate, but for the moment, Alfie was pleased to be reunited with his squadron colleagues. There was little to do during the day except talk, and ponder the character of their fellow prisoners, the French, who already seemed to be more settled and more resigned to their fate. The lights went out at 10.00pm, leaving the prisoners alone with their thoughts.

On each day, Alfie was obliged to attend a morning and evening roll call – the *Appel* – at which the officers and men were paraded in the central courtyard and counted. The French and the British had a very different approach to such duties and at opposite ends of the scale. The British made a point of adhering to the military niceties; the French threw all convention aside and were more a gaggle of dishevelled and disinterested troops than anything that could honestly warrant being called a 'parade'. This changed, however, on the morning of November 11 – Armistice Day. On this particular morning, the turnout from both the British and the French was immaculate. The Last Post was sounded by a bugle that had been secured for the occasion, and Day made a short speech in praise of his Allies and the promise of victory. The Germans, wisely, chose to stay away.

In the second week of December, Alfie's routine was again disrupted. His commanding officer – the senior British officer (SBO) in the camp – was among a party of officers who were told to pack in preparation for a move to a new prison. Mike Casey would be going with them; it would be the last time that Alfie would see his skipper alive. Also selected for the move was Paddy Nelson, who although a humble leading aircraftman, would be accompanying the officers as an orderly. (The RAF insisted on the term 'orderly' in preference to an army 'batman', albeit that the duties were virtually identical.) They did not know it, but their destination was a newly-opened Luftwaffe interrogation centre at Oberursel, the Durchgangslager Luft, or to give it its more common name, Dulag Luft.

The iron beds, however, did not remain empty for long, and with the castle already exceeding its capacity, a number of prisoners – Alfie included – were sent to a hostel in the village. Prisoner ranks had been swelled by survivors from the armed merchant cruiser *Rawalpindi* that had been sunk on November 23. They had a tale to tell of heroism and adventure that eclipsed anything heard until that time.

The SS *Rawalpindi* was a 17,000-ton former P&O cruise liner that had been hastily converted to become HMS *Rawalpindi*, an armed merchantman. The role of the armed merchantman was primarily to intercept and search any vessels attempting to bring contraband goods into German ports; it was not to engage either directly or indirectly with German vessels of any consequence. It was unfortunate, therefore, that the ship should come into contact with two of the Kriegsmarine's very best

– the battleships *Scharnhorst* and *Gneisenau* – from which there was no escape. The Germans signalled that the *Rawalpindi* should heave to and surrender but its captain had other ideas. Rather than turning tail and running, Edward Kennedy (the father of broadcaster and author Sir Ludovic Kennedy) decided to fight, and attempted to engage with his six-inch guns. Before she was able to close the range sufficiently to do any damage, a number of shells from the *Scharnhorst*'s eleven-inch guns smashed into the old liner, turning her into a burning wreck. Within forty minutes the battle, such as it was, was over, and the shattered vessel was on her way to the bottom of the sea, taking her captain and 265 brave men with her. There were thirty-eight survivors in all: eleven were fished out of the sea the following day by HMS *Chitral*; the *Gneisenau* picked up twenty-one survivors and the *Scharnhorst* another six.

Christmas proved a somewhat sombre affair. Alfie had received no news from home and there was nothing by way of a Christmas box to add any cheer. The Germans were still confident of victory and any news that the prisoners did receive of the progress of the war appeared bad.

The New Year, however, brought a further new intake of prisoners; this time the party comprised a number of NCO ratings from two of his majesty's submarines – *Starfish* and *Undine*. Both vessels had been lost within days of one another.

The *Undine* had been the first to go, having attacked a number of boats that its captain thought to be trawlers, only to discover they were German minesweepers. After a short skirmish, a large explosion shook the submarine, blowing her towards the surface and rendering the hydroplanes useless. Without the hydroplanes, escape was impossible, and so the captain gave the orders to abandon ship. The submarine was successfully scuttled, and the crew of HMS *Undine* picked up by her attackers.

HMS *Starfish* suffered a similar fate. She attempted to torpedo a German minesweeper, this time with full knowledge of the type of vessel she was up against. For some reason best known to themselves, the torpedoes failed to leave the torpedo tubes, and the attack had to be aborted. On its second attempt, the hydroplanes jammed, and the captain decided to dive to the bottom to effect a repair. Unfortunately for the *Starfish*, the minesweeper found her and dropped two depth charges but with no result. After a period of silence, and believing the enemy had departed, the captain gave permission to restart one of the motors, at which point a whole series of depth charges began raining down, causing considerable damage. With some areas of the submarine in flood, and no sign of respite, the captain managed to surface and surrender. The ship sank soon after, but all of the crew were rescued.

Alfie was pleased with the company, and the distraction of having new people to talk to. The RAF and Royal Navy prisoners mixed well and within a few days a quorum of them volunteered for a working party that was being organised in Wildflecken, eighty-five kilometres to the south near Bad Sulza. Alfie had in fact approached the SBO before his departure to seek his permission to join the working party should the opportunity arise:

> "No-one could actually make us work, and they especially could not make us if it was in any way helping the German war effort. I had spoken to Day sometime earlier to say that if an opportunity should arise, I would like to go on a working party for it would give me a better chance of escape. And even if escape was not possible, at least being out of the camp gave us a chance of gathering some intelligence that might help others at a later date.
>
> "He gave me his blessing and so at the first opportunity, a contingent of RN Ratings and RAF NCOs and other ranks were sent to work in a camp known as Wildflecken. Here we were put to work on a building site, working on a particular structure that was six storeys high. It was, you have to remember, an extremely cold winter and there was a great deal of ice and snow on the ground. They were difficult conditions in which to work.
>
> "While we were working, we asked the Germans what we were building and they told us it was a barrack block. Since we all felt that building a barrack block could be construed as helping the German war effort, we set about trying to sabotage everything we could. With the ground so hard we channelled the ice and snow into the building's foundations in the knowledge that when the thaw came, the melting ice would damage the concrete and make the building unsafe.
>
> "Remarkably, as far as we were concerned, the Germans failed to realise what we were up to for several weeks, by which time we had done quite a bit of damage. Needless to say they were not very happy with us and told us so in no uncertain terms."

The Germans were indeed far from pleased with the prisoners' antics, and felt that by sending them to another camp, in Weimar, it would serve as a punishment, for Weimar was in the middle of Germany with little chance of escaping. As it was, the plan slightly backfired in more ways than one. Their accommodation, in a stable block on the outskirts of town, was both dry and warm, as was the reception from the local people of Weimar who were much friendlier and welcoming to the prisoners than their previous hosts. For another, they were put to work in a ball-bearing factory, and so promptly stopped what they were doing and refused to work. Alfie, at that time, was the senior NCO:

> "The camp included a number of Polish workers and they told us that we were helping to build a ball-bearing factory. Well we all knew that ball bearings were fundamental to the war effort and so as the senior NCO I was pressed into approaching the German Feldwebel to protest. When I didn't seem to get the answer I was looking for we all agreed to down tools which as you can imagine caused quite a fuss. Rather than confront us on it, they simply moved us to another camp."

The men were only at Weimar for a few days before they were again on the move, arriving first at a small camp in Poland called Schocken (also called Skoki), thirty kilometres north east of Posen:

> "It was called Schocken and it was quite shocking! It had been a working camp for the Russians before we arrived and had three-tier bunks. The conditions, however, as regards sanitation and washing were appalling, with only one tap between hundreds of prisoners."

Alfie did not stay in Schocken for long, however. With the majority of the prisoners, he stayed only a handful of days before yet again being moved onwards, firstly to stay overnight near to a Jewish internment camp, and thence to Posen Fort VIII, one of twenty-four steel and concrete fortifications that circled the town. The reception they received within Posen was among the most hostile that they had received thus far. For the last few miles of their march, the prisoners within the somewhat bedraggled and forlorn column were openly mocked by the Germans who obliged the local townspeople to witness their humiliation, whilst listening to a continuous broadcast reminding them that these were the men who had laid down their arms for Churchill.

Fort VIII was as luxurious as it sounds. It was built in the shape of a pentagon, and the roof was at the same level as the terrain outside. Surrounding the building was a moat and an outer wall, topped with vicious-looking spikes that no man in his right mind would look to climb. Alfie and his colleagues now found themselves in the company of almost 3,000 soldiers of the British Expeditionary Force (BEF) who had been taken prisoner at Dunkirk. For the first time, Alfie realised how lucky they had been by comparison:

"By the time we arrived at Fort VIII, the first of the army prisoners were beginning to arrive in great numbers. They had been forced to march many miles, and some of them were in an appalling state. All of them were exhausted, and some wounded with bloodied bandages around wounds that were clearly in need of attention. It seemed that during the march they had been given little or no food, and what they did have had been taken away from them. They also had no water, and had been made to drink dirty water from a ditch and so dysentery was rife. They looked awful.

"We did what we could to help. We had a little soap between us and shared it with them, trying to help keep them clean. They would strip off their battledress and underclothes and use our razors to remove their body hair to get rid of the lice."

Despite their parlous state, few if any of the men in Alfie's opinion had given up the fight. Some, in fact, already had plans to escape. One was Ron 'Gunner' Gunton who had been shot down on the night of October 15/16 (within hours of Alfie's own misfortune). His crew had been unlucky. Having set off on a Nickel raid (ie to drop leaflets) they had failed to hear a recall message and ploughed on alone only to be shot down for their efforts, their captain being killed. Perhaps it was this sense of injustice that prompted Gunton to make an early bid for freedom. With three others, a rope ladder, and considerable nerve the four of them managed to cause the Germans some consternation before all finally being recaptured – in Ron's case after some three weeks on the run. The method of escape was such that Ron attempted to repeat the exercise some time later, only to be defeated by the weather. It was a sign at least that the fight was far from over:

"There were only twelve airmen and twelve naval men and c3000 soldiers at the fort. Corporal 'Gunner' Gunton got into the centre of the fort where they found an air vent and managed to find an exit to the rear of the fort where there were no guards. Three of my people got out.★ At *Appel*, the Germans laughed as there were three missing. So they counted again. Then it dawned on them that the

---

★One of the three was Sergeant 'Spike' Springett, who had been one of the seven to broadcast messages home on Berlin radio. The third of the RAF men was Aircraftman Paddy O'Brien.

contingent of air force men was smaller. So they hauled me out and demanded to know where they had gone. I said we did not know.

"They took me and two other airmen over the drawbridge and faced a brick wall. We heard them call out the guard. The guard paraded in front of us. They were ordered to load. Then they were ordered to fire. I thought we were all dead, but all we heard were the clicks. We were marched back into the camp and our bread ration was cut. The RAF contingent was then told that we were going to Barth, and the naval men were off to a Marlag [Marinelager]. It taught me how to survive a mock execution. This is when I felt most in danger."

Alfie's time at Fort VIII was comparatively short. While the men had been freezing and contemplating where the next hot meal might be coming from, the Germans had been busy, making ready a 'special' camp – a Stalag Luft.

CHAPTER FIVE
——MAN OF CONFIDENCE——

A Stalag Luft was a camp run by airmen, for airmen, administered solely by the Luftwaffe. It was said to be the original idea of Hermann Goering, the Luftwaffe chief and former First World War fighter pilot who still cherished a somewhat warped sense of chivalry towards fellow airmen.

Stalag Luft (Barth) was situated to the north west of the town on the Grabow inlet of the Baltic Sea, west of Stralsund. Barth was a largely unremarkable place, with a population of a little over 12,000, and if it were noted for anything, then it was its shipbuilding and cabinet-making industries. It was also known for its church, remarkable for its large spire and its architectural ugliness, a true blot on an otherwise grudgingly beautiful landscape.

The prison population was being drawn from virtually all of the camps then in existence, and many of the airmen found themselves reunited with friends they had already made. These 'purges' as they came to be known, were not uncommon, and would continue for the remainder of the war. Sometimes they were used simply to spread the load, and ensure all camps had their fair quota of men to look after. On other occasions they were used deliberately to disrupt potential escape attempts, and break up relationships with prison guards that may have become too comfortable and potentially compromising. On this particular occasion, however, it was to fulfill the promise of having all RAF prisoners – whether officers or NCOs – in the one camp under the same roof.

Alfie and his comrades had been herded onto a train at Posen for the journey to Barth and then marched from the local railway station to the camp. Indeed the idea that they 'marched' is perhaps a little overstated, for by the time they arrived they were both tired and hungry, and trudged the final yards along a dusty road that Alfie remembers ran parallel to a huge field of cabbages. They were among the very first prisoners to arrive, and went through the now familiar process of being counted before their escort guard were finally dismissed, doubtless to enjoy what little delights the town had to offer. As if from nowhere, food in the form of watery cabbage soup and a small piece of bread was distributed to each man, issued with their mess kit – eating irons, an enamel mug and a bowl – for those that did not already have them. There was then an interminable wait as a Luftwaffe Hauptmann (captain – equivalent to an RAF flight lieutenant) and a team of interpreters checked and re-checked the identities of each man before they were taken to an ablutions block for a shower, during which time their clothes were deloused. For some, this was the first hot shower they had enjoyed for many weeks, and the sensation was one of luxury. Suitably cleaned, and with their uniforms returned, they were at last allowed through the main gate and into the central compound

Alfie and his fellow prisoners had arrived within the first few weeks of the camp being officially opened. As such, some parts of it – and notably the officers' compound – were not yet finished. Barth had two compounds – one for officers and one for NCOs – both surrounded by the now familiar double barbed-wire fences and sentry towers. The Germans might later be short of war material, but they never seemed to go short on barbed wire. Within the NCO's camp Alfie made for one of the three barrack blocks, which in turn was divided into rooms of various sizes to accommodate up to twenty men, and threw his kit onto one of the bunks. He then spent time exploring his new surroundings: each barrack had its own kitchen, an ironic facility given the poor quality and inadequate quantity of food that they had so far been given. Outside, in a building that ran at right angles to the barracks, were the toilet and washing facilities. Prisoners were able to access cold showers at any time, but hot water such as he had already experienced, was only available in what was known as the *Vorlager* – a 'sub' compound on the outside of the main compound that contained areas such as the guardhouse, the camp hospital, the fuel store, and the detention cells known, universally, as 'the Cooler'.

What was immediately different in this camp compared to the others was that their jailers were all Luftwaffe men. Naturally enough, these were not the highest quality front-line troops. Many were of a certain age and had been called up from the reserve. Most expected the war to be over quickly, and saw their present occupation as a minor interruption until such time as the British finally saw sense. As such, few were hostile to their captives, the majority benign, and a sufficient number might even have been considered friendly. At least while the war was still going Germany's way. What was common across the board was that they tended to be very 'correct', in the best German tradition, and although conditions were difficult, they were by no means harsh. Correct military protocol and tradition were the order of the day, and prisoners were allowed to a greater or lesser extent to retain their dignity.

Not long after Alfie's arrival, and with the crops on the surrounding farms still in the fields, the NCOs were asked whether they would help with the harvest. Whether the Germans were being intensely naïve, or just unbelievably dumb, is difficult to tell, but needless to say the prisoners leapt at the opportunity. Until that time, many of the airmen had concluded that the best chance of escape was from outside of the prison grounds. It required no tunnels to be dug, guards to be bribed or fences to be climbed. It was merely a matter of creating a diversion, and slipping away at the appropriate moment. There was also another reason: prison rations – which were meant to be the equivalent given to 'depot troops' of the enemy power – were still woefully inadequate, and the airmen knew that rations given to workers on farms were infinitely better, and more regular, than rations inside the camp. They were also, crucially, issued in bulk. There was thus both a pragmatic and potentially heroic reason for going.

Came the day that the rations arrived, a mass exodus of prisoners occurred, fully fortified and buoyed up with the prospect of freedom. Most, not surprisingly, were rounded up within a few hours of their escape, with every part of German life from the SS to the elderly reservist out looking for them. They paid for their sins with an immediate transfer to another camp, Lamsdorf Stalag VIIIb, which was considered – like all of the camps in the Germans' minds at least – escape proof. (Several RAF men changed identities with soldiers so that they could go out on working parties on the basis that they possibly offered a better chance of escape.)

Strangely, and despite the prisoners' efforts, the Germans did not ban all external working, and a succession of prisoners tried their luck when the opportunity for escape presented itself again. None were successful; all spent time contemplating their misfortune in the Cooler.

———————

Christmas at Barth – Alfie's second Christmas of the war – was not the merriest affair. The Germans' attempt at festive cheer was to provide the prisoners with something other than cabbage soup for their dinner. On Christmas Day, held in the main mess hall, each prisoner was treated to a small square of roast pork – perhaps two or three ounces of largely rubbery fat – a spoonful of Sauerkraut and the usual three boiled potatoes. At teatime there was what passed for German 'cake', but which in British parlance was little more than a small slice of rather forlorn-looking pastry. The gloom was somewhat lifted, however, by a Christmas pantomime, and a few drops of weak beer that the prisoners had been allowed to acquire for the occasion. Any volume of alcohol, however, on a hungry and largely empty belly could have a euphoric effect.

It was now more than fourteen months since Alfie had taken off from the grass airfield at Étain and so much had happened in that time. He had already been held captive in six different locations and experienced various depravations that he could well do without. Communication with home for any prisoner was a somewhat hit and miss affair, and Alfie had only received a handful of messages from home in all that time. That any letters could be sent or received at all was because of the good auspices of the Red Cross.

The Red Cross was inextricably linked with both the spirit and the practical implementation of the Geneva Conventions, one of which dealt with how prisoners of war should be treated. Article 79 of the convention allowed the Red Cross to pass on information or enquiries about POWs. These 'letters' were restricted in the number of words they could contain and had to be about family news only. All messages were despatched to the International Red Cross headquarters in Geneva from where they were sent on to their respective destinations.

Alfie had sent his first letter to Vera not long after being shot down. Since that time he had sent further letters and cards in accordance with the established prisoners' allowance, and what the Red Cross authorities could cope with. For by now there were more than 30,000 British military personnel in captivity, and the demands upon their time – and their resources – had reached saturation point. Alfie, however, was comparatively lucky: the letters that did reach him were always full of love and news to keep his spirits high. Not all such airmen were so fortunate. It was perhaps still too early for the 'Dear John' letters that would follow later, and that would cause such despair. But news from home could take prisoners in different ways: news of a newborn baby, for example, that they had never seen, and had no hope of seeing for the foreseeable future could drive a man to despair; so too news of family or comrades who had gone missing, perhaps never to return.

Individuals coped in different ways, and had different mechanisms for handling both the stress and the utter tedium of prison life. Every day, however, had its routine, and at Barth as with every other prison camp this started with the *Appel*.

Just before eight in the morning, a German guard would noisily thud down the corridor of each hut, offering the rallying cry: '*Alles raus. Appel.*' (Everybody out. Roll call.) The men would begin slowly to rise from their beds, not too quickly for they had little to rush for and a whole day to fill. There was also a reluctance in those cold wintry months to leave what little warmth they had managed to accrue throughout the night, and since most men slept fully clothed, there was not even the momentary distraction of getting dressed. The men would take it in turns to act as orderly, trudging over to the cookhouse to collect what passed as breakfast – a scalding hot jug of Ersatz. The last of them would get down from their bunks, taking care not to put a boot in the head of one of their roommates as they descended, and drift outside to assemble, standing five deep in a long line.

In the summer months, the men would have the warmth of the sun to bring a little cheer to their gatherings. But in the depths of winter, standing in snow, and with the chill wind from the Baltic stinging their malnourished faces, it was tantamount to torture – a torture made worse by the Germans' apparent inability to count. More than once the Germans would finish their count, and the arguments would immediately begin as the numbers wouldn't tally. And so the men were counted again. And again. Confusion would often be caused by men who were on working parties or in the sick bay, and on more than one occasion the prisoners would attempt to sort out the mess themselves, or else risk freezing in the snow. Ultimately the farce would end, and the men were dismissed to do as they wanted, which started almost always with 'the morning circuit' – a walk around the camp perimeter, and always starting to the left.

On the circuit, small groups of friends would congregate, not necessarily to talk – for there was little left that hadn't already been said – but at least to share the drudgery. The ground underfoot was hard, not only in the winter, but throughout most of the year, and there was nothing by way of grass to brighten an otherwise grey existence. As the men walked, they passed the guard towers (the so-called 'goon boxes') and were eyed suspiciously by their captors who were ever alert to an attempt to cross the warning wire. Anyone doing so could be and almost certainly would be shot on sight, and there were rumours of rewards and even promotion for the guard who carried out his orders to the letter. There were warning signs attached to the wire that might have been funny in another life. One such sign at Barth read: 'Danger of Life. We shoot. We shoot without warning or call whenever you touch or surpass wire or pole.' Another said simply: 'On trespassing of the wire it will be shot.' No-one ever saw getting shot as being funny.

With the circuit completed, the men would gradually return to their huts, some to retreat to their bunks, others to take their toilet. This might sound a rather middle class, civilised affair when the truth was somewhat different. By way of a latrine the men had what some referred to as 'the Fairy Glen', a large wooden building that sat upon a deep concrete-lined pit. Along each wall of the building ran a bench punctuated with portholes about a foot across, and closed and opened by way of a wooden plug. Here the men would congregate to empty their bowels, not that there was a great deal to empty. Every prisoner, in time, lost any embarrassment that they may have had prior to coming into the camp; sharing the act with 150 or so others at a single 'sitting' tended to wash away one's inhibitions, as well as one's natural waste! Indeed for some, the 'meeting' became one of the social high points of the day, an opportunity to sit with friends and put the world to rights. There was, of course, no such thing as a chain, and it was sometimes amusing to watch newcomers still reach behind them to pull the non-existent cord. The smell tended to be a problem, as did the supply of paper. Much of this was 'adapted' from a weekly news sheet that the Germans had taken to distributing called *The Camp*. The content, one contemporary of Alfie's said, may have been poor, but the texture was perfect!

As far as was possible, Alfie remembers, the men would make themselves busy – busy learning a new language or a new skill, or busy with sport or a pastime:

> "If you kept busy, you got by. In a camp with so many people, not everyone was a career airman like me. We had a good many professionals, those who had been in the volunteer reserve (VR) for example, with peacetime occupations so they laid on lectures and talks of their various subjects such as accountancy and the law. Even the regulars often had a hobby, and so as the months went by we had things like a motor club (sadly with no motors!), an arts club, a music circle, a stage and theatrical society, and of course every kind of sports club imaginable, from football and rugby, through to basketball and cricket."

It was the men who went back to bed that troubled Alfie the most. As one of the first to be imprisoned, he understood better than anyone the need to keep both the body and the mind active:

> "We were always interested to see the newcomers coming into the camp. They soon settled into the activities and very soon came to forget that they had been shot down. But not all. Some woke up in the night screaming – especially those whose aircraft had been shot down in flames or their friends killed. These men would sometimes find it difficult to settle in, and it was left to people like me to get them out of bed and to get involved. Often it would only take a day or two and they would be back to normal."

Such 'normality' is a difficult concept to grasp, more than seventy years after the event. Many of the first airmen to be shot down were indeed regulars, who naturally slotted in to service life, and a prison camp was almost like an extension of what they had been used to – albeit a more extreme version. But as the months and the years progressed, the dynamic of the prison population began to change. Many of those who were shot down were mere boys, who had joined up because of the excitement of flying and a desire to fight for their country. And because the uniform attracted the girls. The traumas they had been through, seeing their friends killed, hearing their screams on the intercom and yet not being able to help, haunted them and left them feeling bewildered and powerless. On capture the Germans would tell them 'for you the war is over' and for some there was relief that they had survived. The war for them was indeed over, and they no longer had to fight. It was not a surprise, therefore, that some were inclined to give up the fight altogether, and plunge into despair in an alien world of which they had no possible comprehension.

There was no certain way of telling how a man would react to imprisonment, in much the same way as there is no way of knowing how a man will react to war, unless and until he has been tested under fire. Those that were married invariably behaved differently to single men, so too those with children, but it was not always as simple as that.

Mid-way through the day, the men would again take their bowls and spoons over to the cookhouse where they would receive their cabbage soup or, if they were lucky, a thick brown slop known as 'Forces Soup'. Once in the proverbial blue moon there might be a thick purée of potatoes in which some pork fat had been boiled, and the men coveted such dishes greedily. With their lunch completed, and the prospect of a long afternoon stretching out in front of them, some of the men would attempt to doze in the hope that sleep would make the end of the day come nearer, and that might be one day nearer to freedom. There was also an obvious physical need to sleep. The calorie content each man consumed left even the fittest and strongest feeling weak and lightheaded. Sleep helped preserve what little energy the men had, and also took away the conscious and continual thought of food.

Some time in the early afternoon, the men would receive their 'dry rations' comprising about five ounces of bread for each man. This meant seven or eight men sharing a single loaf and dividing it equally. Each group of men had its own way of ensuring fair treatment. It was not just about being fair; it was also equally important to be *seen* as being fair. One favoured technique was for each man in the group to take it in turns to divide the spoils, and whoever was in charge of the knife had the last pick. The bread was often accompanied by a spoonful of what the Germans laughingly called 'jam' but was almost certainly chemically created, and 'cheese' from an ingredient that had never once in its life been anywhere near a cow. Very occasionally there was a tiny portion of sausage. The secret, again, was to make the repast last as long as possible until at last it was time to return to the cookhouse for yet another bowl of tasteless liquid that masqueraded as supper. Shortly after, a group of armed guards would enter the compound and the shouting would begin again for the prisoner to assemble for their evening *Appel* – an exact replica of what had gone before. The men would return to their huts until the lights in their rooms were extinguished and the shutters on the windows closed, and each man was left alone with his thoughts.

Some dreamed of friends they had lost; many dreamed of home and their loved ones; all dreamed of food; some swore they could not remember their dreams for they were too disturbing and did not want them to be recalled. A few, only a small handful at first, dreamed of one thing and one thing only: escape.

———————————

Even the most optimistic prisoner recognised that his incarceration was likely to be a long one. With the camp population growing, organisation was key. In the officer's camp, there was a natural chain of command based on rank. Wing Commander Day, for example, had assumed command as the highest-ranking British officer (the SBO). He would automatically forfeit this role should a higher-ranking officer arrive. But amongst the non-commissioned officers, there was slightly more of an issue. To begin with, a group of senior NCOs had attempted to administer the camp according to Kings Regulations and Air Council instructions. Not surprisingly this proved both unpopular and ineffective. It failed to take into account the dynamic of the prisoners who were far from all 'regular' airmen and had little intention of being told what to do. It was decided, instead, that the prisoners should elect a council, and at the head of the council should be a leader in whom the prisoners would have absolute trust. The leader they chose was James Deans.

> "We had started off at Barth with the senior flight sergeant taking charge of the camp, but he was useless. Fortunately he was posted away to Lamsdorf and so we looked around for a camp leader. 'Dixie' was the leader in our block and when the previous incumbent went, everyone said well 'Dixie' speaks German, he looks after everyone, and he is the leader we want. It went to a proper ballot and he received all but a handful of votes. He was invited into our small room."

Deans, who inevitably found himself attached to the nickname 'Dixie' after the international footballer, was a Scot, who had been born in Glasgow in 1914. After schooling at North Kelvinside Secondary School he joined the RAF in 1936 and qualified as a pilot – one of only a handful of sergeant pilots in the air force at that time. When war came he was flying the twin-engined Whitley bomber (what some ironically referred to at that time as Britain's 'secret weapon') with 77 Squadron in Linton-on-Ouse.

Dixie rapidly became one of the squadron's most successful and experienced pilots. Indeed his record of operations is a fascinating snapshot not just of the raids being carried out at that time, but also of the difficulties the night-bomber squadrons

Dixie with an unknown Kriegie and Alfie. Boxing Day, 1942.

faced in those early days of the bombing campaign: synthetic oil plants and storage facilities; aircraft factories; ports and harbour installations. Three attacks on the Kassel aircraft factory inside a week illustrate the challenges the bombers had in finding and destroying important military objectives. Not unusually, Dixie would be obliged to bomb from low altitude, sometimes as low as 5,500ft. Aircraft and equipment reliability were often more of a concern than the enemy defences, although Dixie had his fair share of scrapes with enemy fighters, including two over the city of Turin on the night of August 26/27. He was only a few operations short of completing his first tour when he took off from Linton-on-Ouse on the night of September 10, 1940 to attack Bremen. The primary target was the railway station. He didn't come back. Hit by flak, the aircraft came down at Venebrugge in Holland, and the entire crew was captured.

Deans had a natural air of authority beyond his years that cannot be taught. His tact and diplomacy was entirely natural, and although a regular was able to transcend all RAF 'types'. He also had a practical advantage in that he could speak German, and the Luftwaffe were happy to liaise with him as what they would call a 'Man of Confidence' (*Vertrauensmann*).

With his right-hand men in place, Deans immediately set about bringing new order to the camp. That is not to say that the organisation within the camp beforehand had been necessarily chaotic, but rather that the steady increase in numbers was creating new challenges. And one of the biggest challenges was how to manage and control the distribution parcels.

From the moment that the first two RAF airmen had been shot down*, the Red Cross had been sending parcels to supplement the rather meagre food rations then allocated to prisoners of war. Later the food situation would become so critical that without the parcels, the airmen would have been in danger – without fear of exaggeration – of starving to death, but in the early days they accounted for a few additional 'treats' and a poignant reminder of home.

The difficulties with Red Cross parcels were many and varied. For one thing, the frequency with which parcels would arrive could not be assured. The phrase 'Feast or Famine' could often quite literally apply. The second difficulty was to whom the parcels should be allocated. For those who had been in the prison camps from the early days, their names were already well-known to the authorities, and personal parcels were steadily getting through. But there were also consignments of non-personal parcels that caused even more of a headache. Should the contents of these parcels be 'pooled' and shared, or should they be allocated on some form of rota system?

Alfie had been associated with this difficulty ever since the first Red Cross parcels arrived at Spangenberg not long after he had been shot down:

"The first parcels from the Red Cross came to Spangenberg in December 1939 and I was tasked with going down to the railway station with a couple of colleagues to supervise their collection. I believe we had a handcart on which to load the packages and transport them back to the castle, and I distributed them to my fellow prisoners. From that moment I was connected with the Red Cross until the end of the war.

"Anyone who was there at that time will remember that day, for it was the best Christmas present we could have ever had. The very first parcels were from Fortnum and Masons, and contained such luxuries as a whole partridge in a tin as well as Irish stew, corned beef, marmite, and a few other essentials such as milk powder, sugar, salt etc.

---

*This dubious honour went to Sergeant G F Booth and Aircraftman L J Slattery of 107 Squadron.

"Only two parcels arrived before Christmas but they were most welcome. It was some five months afterwards at Weimar that we managed to get some more parcels through, by which time things were getting a little difficult. Red Cross parcels took second place to any German post, and so could not be relied upon entirely."

The official average daily food ration for a British prisoner of war in the spring of 1941 as quoted in the House of Commons was given as follows:

—— **MORNING** ——
COFFEE (seven grams)
SUGAR (fifteen grams)
HONEY (twenty-four grams);

—— **MIDDAY** ——
BEEF (seventy grams)
FRESH BEETROOT (350 grams)
POTATOES (1,000 grams)
FLOUR (ten grams)
SALT (fifteen grams);

—— **EVENING** ——
COFFEE (seven grams)
SUGAR (fifteen grams)
BREAD (300 grams)
FAT (twenty-five grams)

The truth was of course dramatically different, as attested by the poor health and lethargy of its recipients. While the first few parcels did indeed become the stuff of legend, subsequent packages became more predictable, but no less welcome or even luxurious in the minds of prisoners who had had to suffer a diet of sour bread, bad potatoes and watery soup for many months.

Each non-personal parcel weighed about ten pounds and the contents were largely the same:

A QUARTER POUND OF TEA
HALF A POUND OF TINNED BUTTER OR MARGARINE
A TIN OF MEAT-LOAF OR BACON
A QUARTER POUND BLOCK OF CHOCOLATE
A TIN OF CONDENSED OR DRIED MILK
A PACKET OF RATION BISCUITS
SUGAR
CHEESE (that could trace its bovine heritage!)
and SOAP

The personal (ie 'named') parcels varied depending on an individual's request, and did not only contain food. Extra clothing, for example, was always in great demand, especially given the freezing conditions:

> "In the parcel system, every three months we would get a personal parcel from home – our parents would send us something – an essential pullover or a bar of chocolate. Our clothes would very quickly become ragged, especially as we did everything in them, and so the parcels were not just important for food. We washed our clothes in cold water most of the time, and our Great Coats were never far away when the weather became cold.
>
> "My father delivered post to the Earl and Countess of Shaftesbury (Anthony Ashley-Cooper and his wife Lady Constance Sibell Grosvenor) who frequently enquired into my well being and struck up a correspondence. I said that one of the biggest trials was not having any music to listen to. In one of the subsequent packages I received she sent us three new gramophones and a selection of records, including a copy of the nutcracker suite. For a short time I was the most popular NCO in the camp!"

The gramophone was to have greater significance, of which more later.

The International Red Cross together with the International Young Men's Christian Association (YMCA) could not do enough to help. Almost every demand was met, even for the most (seemingly) obscure requests: for the sportsmen footballs, rugby balls, and cricket bats were all forthcoming. It seemed that no request was too unusual or too difficult. The bookworms in the camp asked for particular books, and although they may take many months to find, and the condition was often far from perfect, find them they did. Under 'Dixie' Deans, a number of committees were formed, and representatives appointed to take care of entertainments, education, repairs, and catering. The committees would meet every month to discuss any key issues and how they might be resolved. The IRC and the IYMCA played their part here too. The entertainments committee needed scripts, props and wardrobe in order to put on an increasingly ambitious array of plays, pantomimes and reviews. The musicians needed instruments. The education committee sought schoolbooks and examination papers to increase the prisoners' knowledge and learning, and to attain real qualifications and degrees. At one stage, even, the Royal Horticultural Society (RHS) sent seeds to the would-be gardeners to do what little they could given the conditions they faced.

Camp life began to find a new order at Barth, and many of the lessons learned would be translated in later camps. But that's not to say there was total harmony. It was not uncommon for a petty argument to spill over into something more violent, although the energy required for violence would soon exhaust both parties. The biggest scope for disagreement was always over food, and this is again where the issue of the Red Cross parcels became prominent.

Among the committees established by Deans was an escape committee. The NCOs, for reasons best known to themselves, called the committee 'Tally Ho' – the cry of the hunter and popular shout amongst the fighter boys as they went into attack. Tally Ho was a mirror of the officers' 'X' organisation. Early escape attempts had been poorly organised and even more poorly executed. Indeed to suggest that they had been organised at all would be a considerable overstatement. What happened in reality was that a few isolated pockets of men would choose to escape, and do so without reference or thought to their fellow prisoners. It was little surprise that they didn't succeed. Deans, with his cohort of helpers – Alfie among them – sought to devise a more co-ordinated, structured approach to escape. He recognised that for an escape to be successful, planning was key, and planning required greater collaboration between the interested parties.

This could take many forms: it could mean greater co-operation in the 'barter' system with guards, using what limited resources they had to better effect. (Un-pierced tins of food, for example, were a most useful currency although Alfie would say the Germans would do almost anything for a bit of Fruit and Nut!) It could mean more co-operation in sharing 'kit', since there were, by now, a growing number of disguises and tools being fashioned to help with each escape, and specialists such as cartographers and forgers (one was a distinguished heraldic painter in happier times) were beginning to ply their trade; it could mean greater co-operation in sharing intelligence, since the greatest barrier to a successful escape was understanding what lay immediately beyond the wire; and it could mean the sharing of food – and it was this that was potentially the most controversial.

The Red Cross parcels contained foods that made life more bearable for the prisoners, and also did wonders for morale. But escapers needed energy to escape and provisions to sustain them for what could be several days on the run. That meant a proportion of the food being allocated to escape, either for the escape itself, or to be used as coercion, and that did not always sit comfortably with the rest of the prisoners. A great deal has been written after the event of an officer's duty to try to escape, but the men in the NCOs compound were not officers. Was it then the expected duty of any serviceman, captured in action, to try and escape? Was a soldier, sailor or airman who did not attempt to escape therefore failing in his duty? Such hypotheses are of much interest today, but did little to trouble the majority of prisoners at the time. Alfie, as a *Vertrauensmann*, had effectively given his parole, as had Dixie.

Many prisoners felt that they had already done their bit, and now it was somebody else's turn. And who could blame them? Some were pragmatists, and knew that for one of many reasons they were simply not suited or equipped for escape, or simply did not have the desire. Flying an aircraft was one thing and took a particular kind of courage; finding yourself alone and on the run in wartime Europe took a different kind of courage and mental attitude altogether. The majority would not stand in anyone's way, but a significant number disliked their own lives being impacted by what they considered the futile efforts of others. They were certainly unhappy at having to surrender their food.

Behind the scenes, further organisation was taking place that would assist with escape. Before hostilities had begun, certain airmen had been trusted with a code (or some have said a series of codes) to be used to communicate with home should they be shot down and survive. It was figured that if a sufficient number of men were so informed, then the odds were that at least one of them would make it to a camp, and a line of communication could be established. Little by little, therefore, messages began to leave Barth that might be considered of military value. Requests for certain items of material were also made. Alfie was not part of this code system, but certainly knew of its existence, and dealt with its implications, for nearly all of the material that was sent for could only come into the camp one way: and that was via the parcels office.

It is important to stress that the Red Cross themselves were not party to any of the prisoners' shenanigans, and without Alfie – and without Alfie's consummate skill in engaging with his German hosts – none of the items would have made it into camp, and few if any of the escape attempts could have been tried:

> "We had a series of codes, so if there were anything we wanted we
> used letters to get a message out. It limited the amount of personal

content you could include in your letters but the Germans never
guessed what we were up to."

The organisation that had been set up in the UK to assist with escape and evasion
was MI9, and it was this obscure branch of the British government that found ways
of communicating back to the camp to inform them that a 'special' package was on
its way. More often than not, the parcels would contain fictitious manufacturer's
names – evident to Alfie, but not so obvious as to arouse the unwelcome attentions
of the Germans. But there was a problem. Every package that came into the camp
was subject to a search. And there was a further difficulty. The Germans had got
wind of news that their own prisoners, in POW camps in Canada, had had their
parcels vandalised insofar as all of the tins had been pierced. In retaliation, the
Germans began piercing the tins in the airmen's parcels. This was a nuisance –
especially since they were heavily relied upon both as 'barter' and as provisions for
escape. Alfie saw to it that some of the tins passed through without detection.★ But
the principal problem still remained: how to remove the contraband items from the
'special' packages without the Germans noticing anything was amiss? This is where
Alfie's skill, guile and nerve came to the fore:

> "I was one of those known as a *Vertrauensmann* – a Man of Confidence
> – but actually I was more of a Confidence Man. I would be told
> by one of the members of 'Tally Ho' to look out for a particular
> package that contained a particular item. All of the parcels would
> arrive at a parcels' office in the *Vorlager*, and I would be escorted
> across with one or two other helpers to sort them out.
>
> "When I had identified the specific parcel in mind, we made up
> various ruses to distract the *Postens* (guards). Sometimes, perhaps,
> we might start a silly argument. Other times it might be as simple as
> distracting them with a smoke or a piece of chocolate. Then I would
> extract the contraband item from the package and hide it about my

------

★Ron Mogg, a fellow Kriegie described Alfie as 'amiable and unruffled' but very much on the ball:
"Fripp was playing an important part in the Red Cross store. He supervised the distribution
of parcels to the British NCOs while the German staff kept an eye on him. Alfie could charm
the birds out of the trees, so it was not surprising that a proportion of un-pierced tins made
their way into the hands of the escape committee, even though the Germans had strict orders
to prevent this because they knew whole tins would be used for escape." (*The Sergeant Escapers*)

Top left: Alfie's mother and father on their wedding day.

Top right: Alfie as a toddler (on stool) with his mother and siblings.
Above: Halton Brats!

Above: Physical education was an important part of Halton life. Alfie is second row, centre.
Left: Hamming it up for the camera.
Below: Halton boys out of uniform for a formal portrait. Alfie is seated far right.

Above: Flying experience. Budding airmen eagerly await their first flight, Alfie seated.

Left: Alfie's skipper, Flight Lieutenant 'Abie' Abrams with his white dog who was often on parade.

Below: Alfie and Alex Logan before the war. Alex would later come off second best to a German fighter and lose a leg in the process.

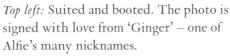

Top left: Suited and booted. The photo is signed with love from 'Ginger' – one of Alfie's many nicknames.

Above right: Alfie during his overseas posting; he described this as the best time of his life.

Above left: A Fairey Seaplane. Alfie searched in vain for an aircraft of this type.

Top: 205 Squadron RAF Seletar, October 1937. Alfie is in the fourth row, sixth from the left. The aircraft is a Singapore III.

Above: Alfie always had a need for speed…

Right: En route to Darwin, August 1936.

Above left: A pre-war portrait of Alfie.

Above right: In flying boats, Alfie would spend hours glued to his wireless set in the questionable comfort of a wicker seat.

Left: Alfie using the camera during his observer training.

Left: Alfie at a wedding in the carefree days before war was declared.

Below left: Alfie and Vera on their wedding day. Only a few days later Alfie was at war.

Below: Alfie set for action with a starter handle in one hand, and cigarette in the other!

These photos show the damage caused
to the Blenheim during Alfie's first crash.
The shattered fuselage is clearly visible
and the force of the crash ripped the
engine and the wings clean off. The crew
were lucky to walk away.

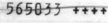

POST ✦ OFFICE TELEGRAM

Charges to pay

_____ s. _____ d.

RECEIVED

1132

_____ m

BM

No. _____

OFFICE STAMP

20 OCT 39

Prefix. Time handed in. Office of Origin and Service Instructions. Words. _____ m

To _____

33

+ 33 11.8 RUISLIP TS 32

FRIPP BERCOS EASTBORO WIMBORNE-DORSET =

UNCONFIRMED REPORT BY GERMAN PILOT STATES YOUR SON
565033 FRIPP LANDED BY PARACHUTE ON GERMAN TERRITORY
STOP TAKEN PRISONER STOP CONFIRMATION WILL BE FORWARDED
WHEN RECEIVED = RECORDS RUISLIP ++

For free repetition of doubtful words telephone " TELEGRAMS ENQUIRY " or call, with this form
at office of delivery. Other enquiries should be accompanied by this form and, if possible, the envelope.

B or C

565033 ++++

Top: Telegram with the unconfirmed report of Alfie's capture.
Above left: A formal portrait of Alfie as a Kriegie.
Above right: Former Brats reunited.

Above left: A German guard checks the contents of a Red Cross parcel.

Above right: Waiting for the mail at Stalag Luft III. This was one of a series of snapshots that Alfie sent home to Vera throughout the war.

Inset: Fort III – a modern-day photo shows the shape and layout of one of Alfie's first prison camps.

Left: Parcel 'Goons' 1939. Food was at the time in plentiful supply.

Top: A cartload of parcels brings cheer to the prisoners.
Inset: Without the Red Cross parcels, the prisoners might have starved.
Left: Alfie on skates.
Above right: The winter weather in the Baltic could be harsh. Kriegies cleared the snow to create ice rinks.

Top left: Alfie overseeing the distribution of the parcels.

Top right: The rewriting of the Merchant of Venice to make Shylock the hero angered their German captors, April 1943.

Above: Prisoners made the best of their captivity, dressed as cowboys for Aubrey Goes West.

Left: Alfie took a hand in producing as well as acting.

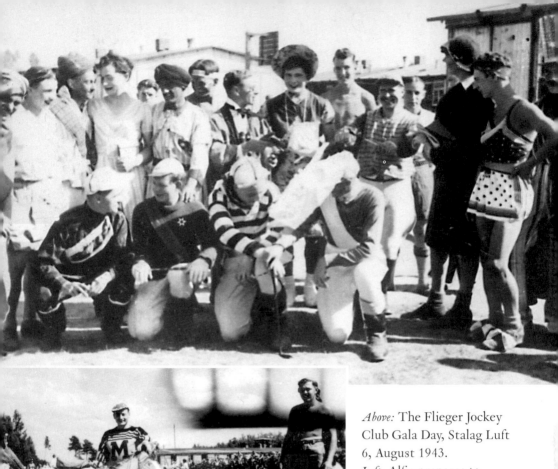

Above: The Flieger Jockey Club Gala Day, Stalag Luft 6, August 1943.
Left: Alfie prepares to mount!
Below: Runners and riders.

Above: Alfie (seated second left) not long after his release. Signals Officers Course, January 1946.
Left: Flight Lieutenant Alfie Fripp, shortly before his final promotion.
Below: Alfie, Dixie and Dixie's wife, Molly, relaxing.

Right: Former apprentices assemble – those who survived the war.

Below right: Alfie represented the RAF at hockey at all levels throughout his career.

Below: Although destined for the air, Alfie's love of sailing never left him.

Bottom: One of Alfie's last appointments, as a flight lieutenant, and the only officer with a flying brevet. (Seated first left.)

Top: Alfie returned to Sagan in 2011.
Above: The official stone used to mark the original entrance to Harry.
Left: At the entrance to Tunnel Harry.

person. I was well in with the guards and the interpreters, and they were always more interested in searching the parcels rather than me as an individual. Once we were done, then we would be escorted back into the camp and I would hand over the illicit goods to my contact.

"We did this at Barth, then at Sagan and indeed at every other camp during my captivity and never once did they search me, and never once did they discover what was going on. In this way a good many items were smuggled into camp, everything from wire cutters to money, sandwiched in-between the two halves of a gramophone record."

Alfie's skill was not limited to trading with the Germans:

"On more than one occasion, the Polish prisoners managed to source all sorts of illicit goods for me. I was happy with that, but told them that I didn't want to know any of their names and they were not to tell me anything about themselves. That way, if I were found out, or any of our goods were discovered, I could not tell the Germans anything I didn't know. With these terms agreed the Poles managed to find everything from maps and compasses to timetables for the local railway and even a belt from a German officer's uniform. On one occasion they even managed to find us some important parts that we needed for the 'Canary'."

The 'Canary' to which Alfie refers was the secret radio, a vital lifeline with the outside world that the Germans knew existed, but could never find. Arguably it might never have come about had it not been for the genius of Sergeant John Bristow. Bristow had been a wireless op/air gunner in 82 Squadron shot down in the disastrous attack on Aalborg airfield on August 13, 1940 when his squadron was effectively wiped out, losing no fewer than eleven out of its twelve aircraft. The officer commanding, Wing Commander Edward Lart DSO, was killed along with nineteen others; thirteen were captured including Bristow, although he was the only survivor from his crew. At first he managed to evade capture and was hidden by a local doctor, but when he learned that the Germans had threatened reprisals he gave himself up. It was his twenty-fifth birthday. (Among the others captured on this raid was Sergeant Donald Blair who went on to write of his experiences as a Kriegie in his book *Clipped Wings*.)

Bristow, the son of an electrical engineer, teamed up with another young prisoner, David Young, a pre-war BBC technician. Young produced a basic wiring circuit whilst Bristow used his scrounging skills to rescue various items from the camp's waste tip. A tuning condenser was made from a mess tin; the transformer was hand wound from wire pilfered from the camp lighting system. Smoothing condensers were fashioned from the tin foil found in packets of cigarettes, inserted between thin India paper (found in an old bible) and soldered at each end. The plastic 'sleeve' was melted wax taken from altar candles. Although the failure rate of such condensers was high (one in four), the ingenuity of manufacture cannot be denied.

The ongoing problem was how to get valves. Everything else could be built from scratch, but valves had to be acquired. Even Alfie's silver tongue was of little use in persuading one of his tame 'goons' to oblige him, and the problem was only solved when another prisoner managed to steal a set from a German radio device when their backs were turned.

If the radio set was clever, the home-made earphones took the prisoners' ingenuity to another level. Crushed razor blades, wire from an electric shaver, more tin wrappers from cigarette packs, a plastic tooth powder container with a hole cut in the lid and a scrum cap were the component parts, which when manufactured made a set of earphones that lasted the war.

The mess tin radio was known as the Mark I; Bristow would later go on to further improve upon his design with the Mark II, hidden within one of the portable gramophones that Alfie had managed to procure from his noble benefactor:

> "The radio was hidden beneath the top plate of the record player, secured by a couple of screws. The radio itself came from the Telefunken company originally, and I recall we altered a couple of letters to let the Germans know what we thought of them if ever the radio was discovered."

News from the radio was not kept to a select few. The camp leadership recognised the vital importance of news to morale, and so a system of dissemination was quickly worked out. A shorthand note of the BBC news was taken each evening, and copies made. Each block was allocated a newsreader (trained by Sergeant Peter Thomas who went on to become a Cabinet minister and a lord), and the newsreader went from room to room while other prisoners stood guard. When the reading was over, the sheets were returned and carefully destroyed. It was essential that no evidence of the existence of a radio set should ever be found. This is how it was that Alfie and the others learned of the conduct of the war, and were able to assess the progress of the various armies on their home-made maps that always showed the German positions, but never the British lines, in case the Germans became suspicious.

It was also how they learned the monumental news that the Germans had invaded Russia in the summer of 1941. 'Special announcements' (*Sondermeldung*) from their German hosts were broadcast over the camp, and for once the Germans' account of the war seemed to match the version reported of the BBC. Morale in the camp fell as the Germans' advance progressed. Tangible signs of victory appeared soon afterwards as the first Russian prisoners began to arrive, emaciated men in rags who had already been forced to march hundreds of miles at the point of a gun. They did not stay; the Russians were not signatories to the Geneva Convention and their prisoners, therefore, were not afforded the same treatment as their British allies. After delousing, they were sent to their own camp, not far away, where they would be set to work as slave labour. Alfie did not dare ponder their fate.

––––––––––––––

Notwithstanding the progress in the war, Christmas 1941 was a comparatively happy affair. The prisoners learned through the Canary of the Japanese attack on Pearl Harbor, and although they could not possibly know the consequences, they recognised at least that they were no longer fighting the war alone. Now they had a powerful ally who could supply them with men, arms and materiel in quantities that the British army could only imagine. Red Cross parcels were in plentiful supply and had been supplemented by special parcels containing tinned cake and plum pudding; the Germans even managed to provide several barrels of beer.

Within the camp the prisoners, Alfie among them, decided to put on a Christmas show, and their version of Jack and the Beanstalk was received with rapturous applause.

––––––––––––––

A large area within the Barth compound was set aside for 'recreation'. That is again a rather grand term for a thoroughly barren piece of scrub on which the prisoners attempted to carve out a variety of different pitches on which they could kick, hit or throw a ball. With the winter 'freeze', the prisoners decided to take this a step further and create an ice rink:

> "I cannot recall who came up with the idea first. It may well have been one of our Canadians for there were by now a few of them in the camp. I know that we had to first approach the camp commandant for his permission and he seemed willing. With so much snow we went out with shovels that had been loaned to us by the Germans and built up the snow around the edges of the football pitch. Then we flooded it. Because it was so cold (in winter at night it could get down to minus 25 degrees centigrade), the

water almost immediately froze and we had an instant ice rink. We requested and were sent ice skates from the YMCA (the skate blades could be easily converted to wire cutters), and soon after we had prisoners skating on our football pitch. In time we were able to make ice hockey sticks, and soon after a number of very competitive ice hockey games were taking place."

Ice hockey, Kriegie style, at Stalag Luft I, February 1942.

The winter of 1941/42 was indeed a cold one and the camp was covered in deep snow. Two enterprising NCOs – Sergeant Johnnie Shaw and Sergeant W L Evans – saw the snow as an opportunity to escape. On the night of January 2/3 they made their way to the cookhouse at eight o'clock in the evening and waited for seven hours until it was time to move. Then they crept down to the wire leading to the officers' playing field and cut their way through, the plan being that they would then be closer to the main outside wire, and freedom. But the escape was to go tragically wrong. Despite being camouflaged with white sheets apparently stolen from the hospital, they were spotted by one of the guards who called upon them to halt. Both men were in the process of standing up to surrender when the trigger-happy *Posten* opened fire, at least one of his five shots striking Shaw in the heart. Deans complained in the strongest terms to the camp commandant that the prisoner was clearly in the act of surrendering but it had little impact. Shaw's body was laid out in a small room at the end of the mess block by the town undertaker and soon after buried with full military honours. After the war he would be awarded a posthumous Mentioned in Despatches, his official date of death being recorded as being January 4, 1942.

There was another consequence to the attempted escape: the Germans were so angry that they put hot cinders on the ice rink so that it could no longer be used. It did not last long. By February the officers in the neighbouring compound were invited over to take on the NCO team at ice hockey. The score is not recorded but the game was played with a rigorous passion that left the prisoners exhausted and all believing they had won something.

Throughout Alfie's imprisonment he was in regular communication with the outside world via the Red Cross. Switzerland was the sole protecting power to ensure the Germans were complying with both the spirit and the actual word of the Geneva Convention. Their representatives were far from fools, and could tell when the wool was being pulled over their eyes. As such they could make life difficult for the Germans and in return, the Germans would make things difficult for them.

The Swedish YMCA, however, also had access to the POW camps as visitors and benefactors, and could let the Swiss know if they detected something amiss.

One of the best known and best remembered was a Swedish lawyer from Stockholm, Henry Soderberg*. It is to Soderberg that Alfie attributes much of the credit for ensuring the safety and well being of prisoners during this time:

> "Soderberg realised there was only so much he could do, but whatever he could do, he did. He supplied us with footballs, cricket bats, playing cards; anything we could not get from England he could get from Sweden and he kept visiting us throughout the war – although the Germans were not always keen. The Swedish realised they were being told a pack of lies. The Germans tried to

---

* Soderberg retired as vice president of SAS and died in 1998.

put on a show but then Soderberg and his colleagues heard our side of the story and found out what was really going on. The YMCA and the Red Cross looked after us whenever they could.

"After the war he ran an airline and Dixie Deans was invited to fly with them (Scandinavian Airlines Systems – SAS)."

Before the United States entered the war, as a neutral country it too took an interest in prisoner welfare and this led to a visit by the American ambassador to Barth. The Germans were concerned to put on a show for such a distinguished guest and saw to it that new clothes were distributed as well as razors and soap and other such luxuries that the Kriegies seldom saw. The prisoners were content enough to use the scrubbing brushes and washing powder that was also provided to clean their huts, and were similarly happy to put on a rather smart parade in front of their bemused German hosts. However much the Germans tried to steer the ambassador away from asking any awkward questions, they could not prevent him from doing so, moving from hut to hut and building a 'true' picture of camp life from the honest answers given by the prisoners. When he had completed his tour, he remonstrated forcibly with the camp commandant, and before leaving presented every smoker in the camp with a quantity of tobacco – tobacco that some prisoners had not seen in months. The mood in the camp notably lifted over the next few days.

The first few months of 1942 were not the best for escaping, the weather was intolerably cold and even the most ardent escapers were content to leave their endeavours until the spring and better weather. There was also an outbreak of typhus being reported as sweeping in from the East, and for once the British and the Germans were united against a common foe. Happily the outbreak did not amount to much in the camp, with only one suspected case being reported.

But events were about to take another turn for Alfie and his fellow NCOs when they got wind that they could shortly be on the move. A new camp was being built at Sagan in Lower Silesia, a camp they were enthusiastically told was 'escape proof' – a challenge if ever there was one to the members of Tally Ho! The usual routine for moving large numbers of men was followed: first they were divided into small groups of around 200 and then divided again and transported in batches via the obligatory cattle truck bearing the immortal legend: forty persons or eight horses. Some wag would normally ask where the horses were going to sit. Moving presented practical issues for the prisoners unable to carry all of their possessions or hard-earned barter. But it also presented an opportunity for escape, and the escape committee was quick to discuss the possibilities.

As they boarded the trucks, a lorry arrived with a loaf of bread for every two men, and the prisoners were also given tinned meats and black potatoes of dubious and probably inedible quality. As the heavy doors slid fast, they knew they were in for a long journey.

The journey to the camp was unrelenting, uncomfortable and unhygienic, and it was a blessed relief when the doors were finally thrown open several days after their departure and the prisoners caught a first glimpse of their new surroundings. With much shouting and gesticulating from one particularly over-excited guard, the men formed into lines to march the short distance to the camp, hidden from view by the dense-wooded area that would later serve as the perfect cover for escape.

Sagan – or Stalag Luft III as it was to be known – was Goering's particular pet project and was intended to house all shot down and captured Allied airman. The Germans, however, seriously miscalculated the numbers of RAF (and later USAAF) men who would be thrown into battle against them, and such camps like Barth that had been closed after the prisoners' departure were obliged to re-open. Accommodation was in the usual barrack-room style, with each hut measuring some 160ft in length by 40ft across and divided in half so as to make two large dormitories. There was neither running water, nor drainage, but there was a small communal kitchen area where tinned food could be heated and water boiled for that very British of rituals, afternoon tea. Alfie shared Hut 102 with 'Dixie' and six others from the inner circle. (Mostly the men were divided into 'combines' of ten though these groups became smaller at different stages of the war. The men would divide their chores, and each group would be allocated time on the cooker that led to some meals being prepared at odd hours of the day or night.)

The area inside the now familiar double barbed-wire fence was a mess from the sandy soil, pine needles and stumps of trees that had been hacked down by the equally ubiquitous Russian labourers to build the huts. Within double-quick time, however, the prisoners had soon organised themselves into their various committees and life began to settle down. Alfie remembers the first few months at Sagan vividly:

> "When we were removed from Barth to Stalag Luft III we arrived after a long train journey to enter a compound that was completely new, and apart from the new buildings and the wire, of course, there was nothing to it. The first people we saw were the Russian labourers who had clearly been put to work cutting down trees so as to clear an area big enough to build a camp.
>
> "The large area within the camp was littered with tree stumps and so we sought permission from the camp commandant to have the area cleared. The Germans would not do it themselves, but

were prepared to provide us with the tools. As a result, we rigged a tripod device and some form of ratchet and pulley system, wrapping the chain underneath the root of the tree and pulling them all out one by one. It was tiring and backbreaking work – particularly for prisoners who were not eating well – but in very short time we cleared enough space to make a football pitch."

With the sporting arena organised, and the summer months approaching, games once again went into full swing, and the prisoners were happy. But they also turned their attention to other leisure activities, and especially the theatre. Acting had become a popular pursuit at Barth, with one production – Aubrey Goes West, a ridiculous western with equally ridiculous outfits – entering folk law for its popularity. Alfie's first acting role was in a similar play, Way Out West, in which he played a cowboy. This was followed soon after by a pantomime in which Alfie took the lead as the dame, ably assisted by Dave Bernard as the fairy godmother! (Bernard had come down on one of the first clandestine operations of the war in February 1941.)

At Sagan, the NCOs managed to persuade their captors to allocate space in one of the huts to be used as a theatre-cum-music hall where they could put on live performances. The Germans eagerly agreed, reckoning that if the prisoners channelled their energies into pursuits such as sport and acting, then their interest in escaping would eventually wane. The NCOs for their part agreed that the theatre would not be used to aid an escape.

With a little bit of Kriegie ingenuity and more hard labour, a pit was dug and an auditorium fashioned at an angle to the stage. Within a very short space of time, the first in a series of concerts and recitals were being given (the instruments came once again courtesy of the YMCA) and a good number of prisoners were putting themselves forward as actors, Alfie among them:

"Not long after we moved into Sagan we thought about a theatre. We dug the foundations and we built a theatre with the Germans' blessing. They assumed it would keep us busy and take our minds off escape. It didn't, of course.

"One of the shows we decided to put on (it was actually in the spring of 1943) was The Merchant of Venice and I remember that it took many weeks to rehearse. The scripts came from the Red Cross and for our costumes, one of the interpreters volunteered to go to Berlin to find them for us. Since the Merchant is a play where one of the central characters is a Jew, the costumes were not much in demand.

"The Germans always made a point of coming to watch our performances and they would always sit in the front row and politely

Aubrey Goes West at Stalag Luft I, 1941.

laugh or applaud at the appropriate times. In the play, the character Shylock, the Jew, is the villain of the piece, lending money to poor Bassanio in return for a pound of flesh if he fails to repay it. I played the part of Launcelot, Shylock's servant. The part of Shylock was taken by Cyril Aynsley.

"We completely re-wrote the script so that rather than being the villain, the Jew became the hero. It took the Germans until about half way through the production before they realised what was going on, at which point they all stood up and marched out in protest. They were not best pleased."

The Merchant of Venice was one of around a dozen plays in which Alfie acted or was closely involved, and which served to keep his mind active and what he referred to as 'disconnected' from the drudgery of camp life. In both the officers' and the NCOs' compounds, Stalag Luft III became the training ground for a good number of young men who were allowed to pool their acting talents and who would later go on to make a name for themselves in post-war cinema and television.

Among the officers, Peter Butterworth, who became best known for starring in the Carry On series of films in the 1960s and 70s, was a particular friend of Alfie's who had served in the Royal Navy and been captured in Norway in 1940. He had escaped from Dulag Luft but been recaptured after three days on the run.*

Rupert Davies and John Casson were also commissioned men who went on to become well-known post-war actors. Davies had been a Fleet Air Arm observer whose Swordfish had come down off the Dutch coast. He made three attempts to escape, none of which succeeded. Casson was also a naval man, in command of 803 Squadron flying Blackburn Skuas from the deck of the *Ark Royal*. He and his observer, Peter Fanshawe, were shot down in Trondheim harbour whilst attacking the German battle cruisers *Scharnhorst* and *Gneisenau* and subsequently captured. Casson and Fanshawe would later play an integral part in the Great Escape.

Among the NCOs, perhaps the best known within the acting fraternity was Roy Dotrice. Roy was a wireless operator/air gunner with 106 Squadron who found himself a prisoner in Stalag Luft III, having been shot down on a 'Gardening' (ie mine-laying) trip and captured in May 1942. Still only a teenager and with a young, fresh face, it was not surprising that within camp he was more often than not given the female leads although, as Alfie remembers, his bandy legs were enough to remind fellow prisoners of his true gender before their imaginations ran completely out of control.

Professional photographs of many of the plays and other leisure activities were taken (Alfie managed to persuade one of the camp interpreters to take a photograph of him in colour) and appeared in German propaganda, giving the impression in Germany – and indeed back home – that prison life was a somewhat gay and pleasant affair. Certainly there was much hilarity to be derived from the Flieger Jockey Club Gala Day complete with jockey's silks and riding britches, and competition was genuinely fierce to enter the NCO's arts and crafts exhibition. The Kriegie's ability to fashion full-scale replicas of famous fighting ships from bones and splinters of packing cases was a wonder to behold.

It was perhaps not a surprise that some in Britain came to misunderstand and misjudge the true plight of the prisoner of war, especially young girlfriends or wives who had only known their menfolk a short while before losing them for the duration. Life could be cruel for both sides and within the camp, a primitive form of relationship counselling service was established to help and advise prisoners work through and resolve their relationship issues. Some would of course receive

---

*While at Stalag Luft III he had been one of the 'vaulters' taking part in the famous 'Wooden Horse' escape, and it was said that after the war he had auditioned for a part in the film of the same name but been turned down because he did not look suitably heroic!

Arts and crafts at Stalag Luft III, August 1942.

the cruellest of news for a man already feeling his youth and his life slipping by with the arrival of a Dear John letter. For the unmarried men this was bad enough but perhaps understandable; for the married men, the strain placed upon them was often intolerable and some would break. At a practical level, it occasionally meant agreeing to a divorce and having to manage the necessary paperwork whilst hundreds of miles from home and no clear idea as to if and when they would ever be coming back.

Fortunately, the prisoners had two of the ablest of men to help them in their hours of need. One was Peter Thomas, the camp's erstwhile news-reading tutor. The other was Cyril Aynsley.

Peter Thomas, a Welshman and proud of the fact, had been reading law at Jesus College when war broke out. Having qualified as a sergeant pilot he was flying as the second pilot with 51 Squadron on the night of June 19, 1941 when his aircraft (a Whitley V) failed to return from an attack on Düsseldorf. Cyril Aynsley was a journalist working on the *Daily Express* before enlisting in the RAF in 1940 and training as a wireless operator. Flying as part of the 15 Squadron crew of Flight Lieutenant R P Wallace-Terry on the night of September 7, 1941, their Short

Stirling was hit by flak during an attack on Berlin and crashed, but not before every member of the crew was able to bale out.*

Thomas, Aynsley and Alfie were all part of Dixie Deans' inner circle of trusted confidants and essential administrators:

> "Dixie was like an 'agony uncle', capable of listening to the men's troubles and advising them, especially on family matters. He worked closely with Peter Thomas and Cyril Aynsley. Peter, who later became a QC and an MP, handled any of the legal aspects, including divorce papers whereas Cyril almost always seemed to say the right thing at the right time and diffuse arguments or fights. I know they did sometimes happen, but I personally never came across any fights in the camps. We were fighting the Germans, and very seldom did an argument spill over into fisticuffs."

Alfie's relationship with his German captors was based on mutual respect and was cordial even to the point of being friendly. Some relationships were more cordial than others, and such 'friendliness' was not extended to everyone. Most agreed with Alfie that the camp commandant, Oberst von Lindeiner, was a gentleman of the old school. He may have been the enemy, but he was most certainly not a Nazi and did what he could to make the prisoners' lives bearable. The *Pour Le Mérite*★ at his throat betrayed a distinguished military career which added to his authority and the prisoners' respect.

His deputy, Major Gustav Simoleit, was similarly humane. He was in charge of the camp administration (the 'official' administration rather that the Kriegie's own brand!) and worked tirelessly to promote a sense of co-operation between the two parties. In this he was supported by Hauptmann Hans Pieber. Pieber's image was far-removed from the Aryan superman his Führer attempted to promote being somewhat thin and weedy, and with thick round glasses. Pieber was noted for his humour, although not all of the prisoners shared in his jokes.

---

*One of those crew members was the navigator, Sergeant Richard Pape MM. Pape was an inveterate escaper and one of the few to make a successful 'home run' by feigning sickness in the autumn of 1944. He wrote about his experiences in the classic account, *Boldness Be My Friend*.
★Known colloquially as 'The Blue Max' – Lindeiner had earned his, and The Prussian Order of the Crown, in East Africa and during the First World War.

The sergeant major in charge of the camp 'Ferrets' – the men who snooped on the Allied prisoners to disrupt potential escape attempts – was Feldwebel Hermann Glemnitz, or 'Dimwitz' as the prisoners liked to call him. Glemnitz was kindly thought upon as a man and was far from dim. His abilities in 'counter intelligence' were both respected and feared in equal measure for Glemnitz thwarted many a would-be escaper's bid for freedom.

Among the Ferrets, two were remembered in particular: Griese and Pilz. The prisoners had no issue with 'Charlie' Pilz as an individual, but his nose for sniffing out tunnels was a constant irritant. Griese, however, was universally despised, and his behaviour much more in keeping with the story-book image of the beastly 'Hun'. Known as 'rubberneck' – both on account of his constant snooping and a physical peculiarity – he was not averse to giving prisoners a clout with the butt of his Lugar if they did not move or respond quickly enough to his instruction. Alfie described him simply as 'a nasty piece of work' – in many ways an understatement about a man who he detested with vigour.

Alfie came into contact with the German administration staff and interpreters on a daily basis and came to recognise and respond to their moods. They were intelligent men, and although they could not, of course, be trusted, they were at least largely predictable. Rather less predictable, however, were the actual guards – the *Posten* as the prisoners called them:

> "The *Posten* had a single-tracked mind. They were second grade and usually not very well educated. But they were very good at obeying orders and doing what they were told. If they were told to shoot a prisoner trying to get over the wire, then they would shoot him. They would even be rewarded for it with extra leave. The others – the interpreters in particular – were far more intelligent.
>
> "How the Germans treated us was usually consistent but did change as the fortunes of war ebbed and flowed. You could always judge how the war was going by the mood of the Germans. While the Battle of Britain was in full swing, and it looked like an invasion of England was imminent, they were in high spirits. They were similarly in high spirits when the advance into Russia commenced. But these moods soon turned and they began to take out their frustrations on the prisoners. Extra *Appels* were called and searches made to punish us. You could feel the tension on the air."

Searches by the Ferrets of the prisoners' huts were a matter of routine and were as much a nuisance as they were a danger. Three years as a Kriegie had taught Alfie and his colleagues the art of concealing contraband that no Ferret could ever find, not unless he got lucky or the prisoners became careless. Entire false walls could be built into a hut, behind which substantial amounts of vital escape equipment could be stored and accessed when needed. 'Snap' searches could cause more of a problem, and occasionally comparatively 'low-grade' contraband might be sacrificed to satisfy the Germans and lead them away from more essential items.

Of far greater danger, and disliked by both the prisoners and the 'ordinary' Germans alike, were the searches that would come later at Heydekrug by the secret state police – the dreaded *Geheime Staatspolizei* (Gestapo). These men were the stuff of nightmares, and would usually arrive in the early hours of the morning, switch on the lights and, if necessary, physically drag the prisoners out of bed and demand they got dressed. After a personal search, the men were then herded onto the parade ground where they would then wait whilst the Gestapo went about their business. This usually comprised smashing up and tearing down everything within a hut in a bid to find something of value that would prove their superiority. The Ferrets and their leader feared the searches almost as much, for they knew that if the Gestapo did strike lucky, and stumble across anything important, then their heads could quite literally be on the block. At the very least they could expect an immediate posting to the Russian Front which by now was no longer a scene of continual German victory. As it happens, the Gestapo never found anything of substance, to the mutual relief of all concerned.

For every measure the prisoners took to outfox the Germans, the Germans devised a counter measure to fight back. To counter tunnelling, for example, the Germans buried microphones into the ground so that they could monitor for any sounds of digging. They dug trenches and flooded areas of ground to deter 'moles' – those inclined towards digging shallow tunnels over short distances for 'blitz' escape attempts. And they regularly moved airmen they suspected of being part of a planned escape to different camps, so as to disrupt their organisation.

The prisoners became more expert as time went on. Tunnels were always popular: at Barth the NCOs dug no fewer than ten tunnels in the space of two years. Unwittingly, the Germans helped in the building of one tunnel in particular:

> "One of the biggest challenges at Barth was how to get hold of the electrical wire for the lighting system in the tunnels. The Germans wanted to put tannoy loudspeakers outside each of the blocks to spread propaganda. These tannoys also had microphones so that they could listen to what we were saying.
>
> "One day an electrician came into the compound and began by drilling a hole through our hut and then started to feed the wire through the hole he had created. When he tried to come into the hut, we delayed him a little. When he eventually came in he realised

that all of the wire had gone. We repeated this exercise several times before he finally gave up. He couldn't say anything or he would have been in trouble. Eventually he came back with an assistant, but by then we had all the wire that we needed."

The pace of tunnel digging was even more frenetic at Sagan. The Germans knew they were digging and became adept at finding the spoil; favourite spots such as above the ceiling or beneath the floor boards were already known. But although they could find the evidence that tunnels were being dug, it was a more difficult challenge to find where the tunnels started.

The prisoners, through the auspices of the Tally Ho organisation, established their own methods of 'security'. Whenever a Ferret entered one of the huts a warning would be given, either by a simple cry of 'Tally Ho' or more usually 'Goon in the block'. The most dangerous Ferrets – those really good at their job – were allocated individual prisoners to watch and follow them as soon as they set foot into the main camp. The NCOs even had a name for the 'watch' system that they devised, referring to the individual Kriegies as 'duty pilots' reporting to the 'duty flight' – ie the main controller. It was even said that the King Ferret would check in himself with the 'duty flight' whenever he wanted to know the whereabouts of any of his men!

Within Sagan, the administrative side of prison life was perfected. Red Cross parcels were in regular supply – as were the 'special' parcels for Alfie to manage. In the parcels office he would occasionally meet with his opposite number from the officers' compound, Flying Officer Marcus Marsh with whom Alfie struck up a particular friendship. Marsh was a fascinating character in that he had been a famous racehorse trainer before the war, training the winner of the Epsom Derby and the St Leger (Windsor Lad) in 1934. He had been shot down in May 1941 over Mannheim while flying with 214 Squadron. It was through Marsh that Alfie learned of the various escapes being planned within the officers' quarters.

The men were comparatively well fed and in good humour. An abundance of cigarettes, chocolate, coffee and other such luxuries were traded with certain German guards in a most organised fashion for items that would ultimately support the prisoners' attempts at escape. Alfie and some of his contemporaries became adept at compromising guards to the point that they became bolder in their requests, managing to secure, for example, parts for a camera and associated equipment on the grounds of wanting to take some 'holiday' snaps:

"The escape committee would make friends with some of the Germans and keep them sweet with coffee or cigarettes so we would know what was going on in the camp. We would attach ourselves to them and no-one else or it might threaten the flow of information. The guards could provide most things: buttons for a uniform; cloth to make jackets or trousers; even a railway timetable. They would not give us anything for our radio sets, but anything else seemed to be OK. Whenever we moved camps, we took with us any of the stuff we had accumulated – depending on how bulky it was. Whoever came in next was left to fend for themselves."

Tunnels were by no means the only potential method of escape. Some of the bolder, German-speaking prisoners and those who had determined to learn and perfect the language during their incarceration soon focused on the idea of impersonating their hosts, and quite literally walking out of the gate in home-made German uniforms. The most spectacular of these – certainly up until that point – was made on the night of December 29, 1942 by two legendary names in NCO escaping circles – George Grimson and Alan Morris.

Grimson had been a prisoner since being shot down in the summer of 1940 during an attack on Hamburg. He was only one of two survivors from his 37 Squadron crew. Morris was similarly one of only two survivors in his crew, after their 77 Squadron Whitley came up short during a raid on Cologne in May 1941. They were shot down by a nightfighter.*

The pair of them devised an ingenious ruse that involved impersonating two German NCOs whom they vaguely resembled. Fully suited and booted in their fake uniforms, and suitably equipped with false papers to confirm their new 'identities', Grimson and Morris used the cover of a theatre production – to which a number of the guards had been invited – to create a diversion and then headed for the first gate. They berated the guard in a dangerous game of bluff and were allowed to pass. At the second gate, the sentry asked them for their numbers. For a moment they were stumped: they did not know that the German security officer had just introduced a new system whereby every guard entering the compound was being issued with a number. They repeated the bluff at the earlier gate, balling out the guard to such an extent that he was intimidated into letting them through. The guard accepted their story that they had been part of a much larger party going to the theatre, and so had never been issued with one. They then left the German compound by an unguarded gate near the officers' quarters and were free. Once safe in the woods they changed out of their uniforms and adopted a new disguise as foreign workers.

---

*Leutnant Kurt Loos of 2/NJG1 for his first victory.

From Sagan railway station they made it as far as Bayreuth, a Nazi stronghold in northern Bavaria. Here their luck finally ran out. Their papers were inspected and they were taking in for questioning. Interrogated, they were eventually obliged to reveal their true identities and were soon after returned to Sagan and the obligatory two weeks in the Cooler.

The escape, even though it failed, was a tremendous morale boost for the camp. This had not been Grimson's first attempt at impersonation and it would not be his last. On his first he had donned the Ferret's white-jacket fatigues that they wore in the summer and with a converted field service cap, German badges of rank, genuine German leather belt and a pistol holder set out to impersonate another German corporal with whom he had a passing resemblance. As with good comedy, timing played a critical part in the success of an escape, and George chose a day when the corporal was away on leave. With a German jam tin that had been re-fashioned as a bucket, and with other plausible accoutrements such as brushes and cloths, he approached the compound gate and was waved through with only a cursory glance at his pass. He then walked across the outer compound and past the camp stores, coal dump and sick bay and went again unchallenged into the German compound. Now came the difficult part: he was obliged to spend the next few hours among the Germans until it got dark and he could slip away. Somehow he managed to avoid all contact with his 'fellow' guards and left through a wicket gate at the side of the German officers' mess. He was recaptured a few days later.

But not every escape involved such planning, or had a (relatively) successful outcome. A less sophisticated attempt by two NCOs in February 1943 ended in tragedy. One night, Flight Sergeant A Saxton and Sergeant Albert Joyce made for a hole just outside the warning wire and within twenty-five feet of the main fence. Joyce took the lead but when he was half way across the compound he was caught in the beam of a searchlight and without warning the guard opened fire. All hell let loose and the camp was suddenly flooded with Germans, shouting and gesticulating wildly. Joyce was mortally hit, and although he lingered in hospital for several months he eventually succumbed to his wounds.*

Morale was a delicate condition that could polarise from deep depression to manic euphoria both at an individual and at a camp level. One of the NCOs actually kept a morale barometer that he would update daily! Escapes were often good for morale;

---

*Saxton had been shot down in October 1941 as part of a 214 Squadron crew, all of whom survived to become POWs; Joyce was a fighter pilot, shot down in his 234 Squadron Spitfire Vb on an escort mission to Brest, December 30, 1941.

the thought of getting 'one over' the Germans and winning a small victory to contrast the defeat of captivity left even the gloomiest of Kriegies with something to smile about. But when an escape went wrong, or a tunnel that had taken months to dig was suddenly discovered, the mood could swing again. Incidents of prisoners being shot whilst escaping were few and far between, but the finality of the act left many wondering whether the price of escape was worth paying. But not George Grimson. And his next escape – in full view of both his captors and his fellow prisoners – was not only breathtaking in its audacity, but sustained camp morale for many months to come.

For some weeks a rumour had been circulating that the NCOs were once again to be moved. Sagan, it appeared, was to become an officers'-only camp. Soon this rumour was confirmed when the Kriegies were told to pack their belongings and prepare to move in stages to a new camp at Heydekrug, further to the east. It would, indeed, be the most northerly and the most easterly of all of the camps that would house Allied prisoners of war, close to the border of Lithuania.

Moving nearly 2,000 men took a considerable time to organise, and those who were escape-minded – like good conjurers – recognised this time as an opportunity to escape while the Germans were, in effect, looking the other way. Busy camps had not only a great many guards but also a large number of workmen tasked with local repairs and maintenance. Telephone systems and electrical circuits were all prone to failure; many of the camps also suffered from poor plumbing and drainage. It was with this in mind that Grimson attempted his most audacious escape to date and, in Alfie's opinion, probably one of the boldest of the war.

The advance party of NCOs was in the *Vorlager*, their kit having already been sent ahead (a symbol of German efficiency!). Now the Germans had to check the prisoners' identities and conduct a final count, before they would be marched away. It was three o'clock in the afternoon of June 20, 1943. Secrecy was crucial, and only a small number of Tally Ho members, and Alfie, knew that an escape was 'on'. The majority paid little or no attention to the German workman with his electrical test equipment and ladder heading towards the warning wire and asking the guard in the watchtower for permission to approach. There were a few prisoners who may have been curious to see this same workman climb his ladder and span the double fence with a short plank, traverse the plank, and then begin to work testing the lights and the electrical circuits with his ammeter. Only the most very observant might have wondered at his equipment; not one would have spotted that the equipment was pure invention, and that for headphones the workman was wearing blackened boot tins over his ears! A dangerous moment passed when a number of 'genuine' Ferrets entered the camp, but gifts of cigarettes and chocolate from the soon-to-depart Kriegies who were in on the act kept them out of harm's way.

The workman continued about his business for more than twenty minutes, moving along the fence to 'test' for any faults in the wiring. It was a tricky balancing act, and it did not come as a surprise to the guard in the tower nearest the activity when the workman dropped his pliers just inside the outer fence. With a certain amount of swearing and cursing in German, the workman indicated that he wanted to go down in the outside of the wire to retrieve his kit, and then walk around the outside of the wire to the gate to get back in. The guard agreed, and the workman climbed down, laughing with the guard as he did so. Retrieving his pliers, he proceeded to walk around the fence, slowly, pausing only to pass the time of day with the guards in each tower as he passed. When he was out of their line of sight, the workman – George Grimson – slipped away into the woods and he was gone. The whole escape had taken just thirty minutes, but to Grimson, and the Tally Ho, it must have seemed like a lifetime.★

The German and British senior staff came out to bid the prisoners goodbye and farewell. Oberst von Lindeiner warned the men (who he referred to as 'his boys') not to try to escape; he genuinely feared for their safety. The SBO from the officers' compound, Group Captain MacDonald, reminded the men to retain their discipline, and never doubt the ultimate outcome of the war. 'Wings' Day, the former SBO, took off his cap and waved.

The prisoners marched out of the camp as though they were at a military tattoo, and were admired for doing so by their captors. While all of this was going on, Grimson was changing into civilian attire and heading for the station. Thus came one of the most remarkable and audacious aspects of the escape. While the prisoners were being loaded onto the train (once again in the obligatory groups of forty plus), what looked like a Gestapo man – George Grimson in yet another disguise – was sipping a beer in the station canteen. Finishing his beer, he too boarded the train, but in a rather more comfortable passenger carriage.

George was not on the run for long but was unlucky to be recaptured. The Germans picked him up whilst looking for an escaped Russian prisoner who had killed one of his guards.

★The Germans never did understand how Grimson escaped. Shortly after he was over the wire, the prisoners asked for their ladder back, suggesting it had been borrowed from the theatre. The Germans never linked the ladder with the escape.

CHAPTER SIX
——THE LONG GOODBYE——

Heydekrug – designated Stalag Luft VI – differed from Sagan in that it had not been purpose built, but rather reconstituted from a military barracks. It was, however, very new: the four long, low accommodation blocks in Alfie's compound had only recently been constructed, and the smell of fresh paint and wood shavings was very much in the air. The rooms were crowded but comparatively comfortable, the men sleeping in tiered bunks with just enough space between them to move around. The wash house and lavatory block were as expected, and at one end of the camp was the kitchen. The camp was under the command of Oberst Hermann von Norberg.

The main party of NCOs had arrived on June 25, 1943 after a long and difficult journey that had been interrupted by a major bombing raid on Berlin. Some of the prisoners could not help but taunt their guards and enquire whether they had any relatives in the city. Alfie chose to remain quiet.

It did not take the prisoners long to take stock of their new surroundings, and they liked what they saw. A few prisoners were already in residence, and were a little surprised to see such a large body of Kriegies appear in one go. No doubt they expected to expand their numbers gradually rather than in such biblical proportions. Their temporary leader was usurped, and Dixie Deans was once again immediately elected camp leader and Flight Sergeant Ron Mogg his deputy. Within a very short space of time the various committees had convened, and Kriegie life continued.

116

The library, church, theatre and university were soon in full swing, and for the sports enthusiasts, there was even a playing field with a few tufts of grass. But the happiest of all were the boys in the Tally Ho. They recognised immediately that the location of Heydekrug presented a real opportunity for escape. There was not just the possibility of a ship to Sweden, but with the advancing Russians, there was now also the chance of heading east.

By the summer of 1943, the war had reached and indeed passsed its tipping point. Rommel and his successors had been beaten and all but kicked out of North Africa; the Russians had taken hundreds of thousands of German prisoners at Stalingrad and were on the advance; and the Allies had landed in Sicily as part of a plan to attack Hitler's 'soft underbelly'. The night assault on Germany by the RAF had been joined in force by the squadrons of the US Eighth Army Air Force and towns and cities in Germany and German-held territories were being pounded day and night. A new mood of optimism was filtering through the camp. The appetite for escape was possibly at its strongest.

Within forty-eight hours of the prisoners arriving, the site for a new tunnel had been found, and digging was underway. Conditions were far from ideal owing to the height of the water table. The danger of collapses were ever-present and frequently dangerous, men sometimes being pulled by their feet to safety with their lungs bursting from lack of air. The Germans had declared Heydekrug to be 'escape proof' and the prisoners were determined to prove them wrong. Motivation was not an issue. The first tunnels, however, were quickly discovered, and the prisoners found in their new camp security officer, Major Peschel, a worthy adversary. As well as 'technical' counter measures such as underground microphones and seismographs, Peschel also turned to more 'mechanical' but no less effective means. One morning the prisoners were somewhat bemused to hear the engine of a large steam roller in full voice, as it wheeled up and down the perimeter fence with the purpose of collapsing any possible tunnels.

But three men in particular persevered led by a Texan flight lieutenant by the name of Bill Ash and inevitably known as 'Tex'. Ash had swapped identities at Sagan with an NCO believing that he stood a better chance of escaping from a new camp rather than staying where he was. As a result he was masquerading – much to his fellow Kriegies' amusement – as Sergeant Don Fair. Ash was very quickly made part of Tally Ho, and started planning a new escape. He recognised, as did many of the others, that most tunnels were detected because the entrances were not properly concealed; looked at another way: spend time concealing the entrance, and the chances of discovery were greatly reduced.

Ash, in consultation with his tunnelling 'team' that included Flight Sergeant 'Paddy' Flynn and Sergeant John Fancy, came up with the idea of starting the tunnel in the washroom, starting from a latrine. The rationale was foolproof: not even the most ardent of Ferrets liked digging around in that much dirt, plus it gave the tuneless scope for shifting large amounts of spoil undetected. They started the tunnel in what was now a familiar pattern, beneath a toilet seat. It was then a precarious walk along an underground brick wall just above the cesspit that led to another underground foundation wall and another hole. Through this hole they carved out the 'chamber' – effectively the start of the tunnel itself. But the rising water created problems from the word go, and they were obliged to re-consider their design. The solution was found by de-constructing one of the hot-water boilers in the laundry room, digging a hole beneath it, and then reconstructing the boiler above it. The ingenuity of the design was such that the men could be digging whilst the clothes were being laundered and the boilers continued to burn.*

Progress was slow but steady. Because they had moved into a new camp, bed boards – which were used as shoring – were in plentiful supply, but falls were still a problem. Nevertheless, within six weeks the tunnel was some 145ft long, about 40ft beyond the perimeter fence. The plan was to reach the trees, but that left a further 90ft still to go. Many within the camp knew about the tunnel's existence, and the excitement at a pending escape was palpable. Indeed it was too palpable, for the prisoners' excitement had been 'sensed' by their guards, and their searches took on a new intensity. The Gestapo also arrived, but besides leaving their usual trail of destruction, they too failed to find anything that could not easily be replaced.

A crisis meeting was called by Tally Ho. The chances of the tunnel being discovered were adjudged to be too great. The dispersal of spoil had become a serious issue with a tunnel so long, and they knew they were chancing their luck to delay any longer than necessary. An early break out was planned, and the forgers, uniform makers and various other tradesmen worked double and treble shifts to ensure everything was ready ahead of schedule. Fifty men were to break out: fifty men requiring identity papers, maps, compasses, food and other essential items to aid their escape. Fifty men whose departure would have to be hidden for as long as possible to give them the best possible chance of a home run.

Finally the night came and the men made their way to the washroom. One by one they climbed down into the tunnel and made their way along its shaft to the exit. At the front, the first of the escapers had broken the surface, breathing in the fresh air that contrasted so sharply with the putrified air in the tunnel created by fifty sweating bodies. The tunnel entrance had been sealed, the trapdoor replaced and ash scattered on the floor to conceal any trace of an escape. It meant the men,

---

*Fancy had been in the bag since May 1940.

however, were effectively entombed in one long coffin.

It was not until around 10.00pm that the first man clambered out of the hole and made for the trees. Then the second; then a third. The remaining bodies in the tunnel shuffled inches closer to wait their turn. The fourth, fifth and sixth man all made it out safely, disappearing into the night. Then the seventh and the eighth. All seemed to be going well. The distance from the exit to the woods was about thirty yards, and by keeping low, and watching for the movement of the guards patrolling some distance away, a mass escape looked on. As the ninth man emerged, however, suddenly it all went wrong and he was spotted. A German opened fire and within moments a party of guards was thundering into the compound and surrounding the washhouse. The men trapped in the tunnel started burying their forged documents any which way they could to prevent them from being discovered.

The camp commandant was very quickly on the scene and a thorough search of the washroom was soon underway. Try as they might, however, the Germans could find no trace of the tunnel entrance. It was only after the tunnelers themselves began scratching at the trapdoor that the secret was finally revealed. One by one the forty or so remaining prisoners were hauled out and dumped in the Cooler.

The Germans, of course, had no idea at this stage how many men had made it out, and the prisoners were certainly not going to help them. At the morning *Appell*, after the Germans had completed their count, it appeared that the total number of prisoners on parade or reported sick was actually in excess of the compound strength. At a further *Appell* there were similarly chaotic scenes, even to the point that the Germans created 'sheep pens' through which the prisoners had to pass and be counted. Tally Ho, however, had for once issued a general order that the prisoners were to do everything possible to disrupt the Germans' efforts which they took to extremes by bringing out stools and piling them on top of one another to create an enormous pyramid and then daring one another to climb to the top. It would be yet another twenty-four hours before the Germans were finally able to ascertain that there were eight men on the loose, but even then they couldn't be quite certain. When they began the painful process of identifying each prisoner by his identity card and photograph, they were thwarted when three or four hundred of those cards 'disappeared' virtually in front of their noses.

Disappointingly, perhaps, for such a large escape, every one of the escapers was eventually recaptured, although at least one was on the run for a fortnight.

Alfie was indirectly involved in this and earlier escapes by providing items of equipment via the 'special' parcels requested by the Tally Ho. He had a more direct role in the next escape, however, although with mixed fortunes for all those involved.

———————

By the beginning of November 1943 there were more than 3,000 prisoners at Heydekrug although the Germans did their best to reduce that number by taking pot shots at the prisoners whenever they went too near the warning wire. Even when they were given permission to cross the wire – usually to retrieve a ball – the prisoners were still putting their lives at risk. The prisoners similarly tried to create space by trying to escape, and despite the dangers, the numbers of escape attempts rose considerably in that autumn and winter. George Grimson was ready for another attempt, but an escape with a somewhat different purpose.

For some time the prisoners had recognised that an escape stood a much greater chance of success if help was available once they were outside of the wire. Ideally, a 'safe house' or perhaps even a network of safe houses and contacts would considerably increase the likelihood of a precious 'home run'. Grimson and Tally Ho now had disaffected Germans on the inside and Polish resistance on the outside who were willing to help, and had learned of a particular establishment, known only as 'The Parson's House', where a friendly reception was waiting for any would-be escaper. Grimson's task was to find the house, and create the network through which future escapees could pass in safety. But first, he needed to escape again himself, and for the third time he used his favourite method, one of impersonation.

The New Year of 1944 was only a few weeks old when Grimson's plan came to fruition. Alfie recalls his part in it:

> "I knew that Grimson was going to make a break for it dressed as one of the guards, but that he needed somewhere to hide and to change. I suggested that the store room would be ideal; it was where we kept the spare Red Cross parcels and food. The key to the store room was closely guarded but I had a copy made so he could use it. As usual, a bit of chocolate and some coffee was enough to keep the guards distracted while we hid the civilian clothes that he needed, and more chocolate and coffee were required to take away his German disguise after he was free."

Some further explanation is required: Grimson's plan was remarkably simple. At the end of an *Appell*, he would mingle with the German guards in a disguise that included a complete dummy rifle and walk with them back to the *Vorlager*, and from there slip away unnoticed. As it was the plan worked like a dream. The afternoon *Appell* on January 21 went on for a little longer than normal until the Germans were at last satisfied with the count. While they counted, Grimson lay hidden, fully clothed but out of sight. When at last the count was completed, he leapt out of bed, slung his dummy rifle over his shoulder and sauntered over to the gate. Twenty guards had come in; twenty-one went out, Grimson being in the first handful to leave.

Once in the *Vorlager* he hid first in the lavatory where he dismantled his rifle, and then walked across to the locked store room using the key that Alfie had made and let himself in. Grimson had agreed with Alfie where his military disguise was to be hidden, and where his civilian disguise would be kept. Changing into his new identity, complete with trilby and forged papers, he then spent what was later described as the longest hour of his life until he could at last walk out the gate, conscious that to spend too much time at Heydekrug station was to invite trouble. His escape went completely undetected, and the following day Alfie and a team of Tally Ho helpers somehow managed to bring the packing cases containing Grimson's German uniform and rifle back into the compound, similarly without being searched. The bluff had worked impeccably. Grimson was on the run; a vital uniform – months in the making – was safely hidden, waiting to be used in the next attempt.

Sadly there is no happy ending to the Grimson story. The detail of what happened when he arrived in Danzig and the subsequent difficulties he faced have been told and retold many times*. He was not able to find the mythical parson, and his contacts – including two German guards who had been 'turned' – were ultimately rounded up and either executed or committed suicide. Several RAF NCOs did, however, follow Grimson in the hope of meeting up and two – 'Paddy' Flockhart and Jack Gilbert (the *nom de guerre* of Sergeant J Gewelber) – made successful home runs thanks to Grimson's help. Others, however were not so lucky, caught up in a dangerous new mood of reprisals and revenge, and 'disappearing' never to be seen or heard of again. The luck ran out for George Grimson too at some point in the spring of 1944. It was not until March 25, 1948, after three years' of fruitless and frustrating investigation, that the Air Ministry certified his death for official purposes as having occurred on April 14, 1944.

For some in the prison camps, escape had been an all-consuming passion. Some Germans, Lindeiner among them at Stalag Luft III, had come to grudgingly admire the skill and audacity the escapers had shown. But not everyone took so kindly to the prisoners' endeavours. Defeat upon defeat in the east had badly shaken the Germans and the once invincible German army now looked distinctly suspect. The night bombing of the German capital and its major cities had erupted with

---

*Full accounts appear both in *The Sergeant Escapers* and Aidan Crawley's *Escape from Germany*.

a new ferocity and intensity, matched only by the German propaganda ministry's ferocious portrayal of the RAF and Bomber Command in particular as *Terror fliegers* – murderers of thousands of innocent women and children. Within the camps, the mood of the German guards was changing too. With every passing news bulletin, the older *Posten* recognised that the end was drawing nigh. He had seen it before. The younger members of the camp staff, however, had never suffered or even contemplated defeat, and began to take out their feelings on the prisoners, with ever-more stringent restrictions and reprisals for even the slightest misdemeanour.

A life-changing order was issued on March 4, 1944, that effectively re-defined the Germans' attitude towards escape. It was known as the *Kugel Erlass* or 'Bullet Decree', and effectively allowed the Gestapo to remove any prisoner of war suspected of taking part in any illegal organisation or resistance movement. The order could in effect be interpreted in any way the Gestapo chose, leaving would-be escapers especially vulnerable, particularly if they were to come into contact with help from the outside. It was this order that undoubtedly did for George Grimson and two other contemporaries of Alfie's during that time: 'Jock' Callander DFM and Warrant Officer R B H Townsend-Coles. It was this same order that also 'excused' the murder of fifty officers who escaped from Stalag Luft III on the night of March 24/25 in the so-called 'Great Escape'.

News of the escape reached Heydekrug soon after the event and was to have a profound effect on camp morale. The German commandant called a 'special assembly' – an unusual if not entirely unique occurrence. For some reason, however, the prisoners – Alfie included – had a sense of foreboding. It could only be bad news. Just how bad, however, none of them could have possibly imagined.

The men assembled and noticed immediately that they were surrounded by a larger than usual number of guards, all of whom were similarly more heavily armed than they had been used to. One prisoner even thought for a brief moment that they were all about to be gunned down. The camp adjutant, Major Heinrich, walked with his head slightly bowed to the middle of the parade ground, followed by the camp interpreter and Dixie Deans. Dixie was out of step with the German officers, as if to deliberately distance himself from what was to follow.

Heinrich announced in suitably sombre tones and in German that there had been a mass breakout from Stalag Luft III. Seventy-six officers had escaped but fifty of them had been shot whilst resisting arrest. Now the reason for the extra German security became clear; they expected – with some justification – a mutiny. For a brief moment there was incredulity among the ranks. Some even thought it was a hoax. Then the full realisation of what they had been told began to dawn on them. Those who were there remember the incident differently. Some say there was silence; others say there were jeers. What certainly happened was that the parade, which was drawn up in three sides of a square, began to close in menacingly on

Heinrich and his interpreter. For a moment, a very real moment, there was danger. A full-scale riot looked possible. Then Dixie Deans stepped in to maintain order, and with a clear instruction the men retreated and the moment passed. Potential bloodshed was avoided.

Everyone knew it was murder. It was only later that Alfie learned that among the fifty was his erstwhile skipper and friend, Mike Casey.

———————————

On June 6, 1944, the news that the whole of the free world had been waiting for finally arrived. The Second Front opened with the invasion of Europe. Now the countdown started in earnest for the defeat of Hitler's Germany. Alfie learned of the invasion through the BBC, but it was essential that the Germans should not know of the prisoners' prior knowledge before it had been formally announced by the camp authorities. But amidst all the excitement there was an element of caution. Plans were put in place to prepare for a German backlash. The radio men set out to build a device that could transmit as well as receive should the need arise to contact advancing Allied troops. But to do so required a particular valve that could only be found in an amplifier kept in the camp theatre. As the theatre was sacrosanct, however, and the prisoners had given their word that it would never be used for any nefarious act, the theft needed to be 'disguised'.

A plan was hatched, therefore, to burn part of the theatre where the amplifier was kept, but leave the majority of the building intact. The ingenious time bomb devised by the irrepressible John Bristow went spectacularly wrong, setting the whole of the theatre ablaze in double-quick time. Firefighters arrived soon after with comical results, one officer looking down the end of the hose as the water sprayed forth into his face. Two Kriegies, Ken Bowden and Jack Lipton, climbed upon the roof of the nearest hut to render assistance, succeeding only in 'accidentally' throwing buckets of water over the hapless guards. It was some time before the fire – and the prisoners' laughter – was finally extinguished.

Rumours once again began to circulate that the prisoners would soon be on the move. Heydekrug, being so far to the east, was now in striking distance of the Russians. For the first time the prisoners could hear the guns, either of the advancing Red Army or the Germans or both. Either way it was the signal to prepare. Alfie distributed Red Cross parcels among the men, advising them on what best to keep, and what could be left. Swag bags and rucksacks were fashioned from towels and blankets, such that when the rumour was finally confirmed, the men were all ready to leave in a planned and comparatively orderly fashion:

"The Russians were getting close and the Germans were terrified. They were using us as hostages. I had by this time about 80,000 parcels in store and went again to Dixie and we decided we would give every man two parcels each and 100 cigarettes. There was a practical reason for this: they could not carry any more and we did not know where we were going. It was quite a burden. Some found it too difficult and ditched their stuff straight away. The Germans said they would send any remaining parcels on but of course they never did."

Heydekrug comprised three *Lagers*, two British and one American, and these were in turn split into two parties of c3,000 men each for their journey to a destination as yet unknown. Alfie was assigned to the first party, led by Dixie, and marched straight to the station without trumpet or fanfare, and with all that they could realistically carry. An uncomfortable and all-too familiar ride in a goods train over several days ended with their arrival at a new camp, and a new number: Stalag 357. Thorn, Poland.

The camp was actually situated to the west of the town, and the men had a long walk from the railway embarkation point to the camp, which had opened in March to house British army prisoners from all over Germany and Austria. It had since been extended to house the new intake of RAF NCO prisoners, and the reception afforded to Alfie and his colleagues was somewhat frosty. Doubtless the army prisoners resented having to share their meagre rations and Red Cross parcels with anyone, let alone men from a different (and junior!) service.

Relationships did not get off to a good start. The soldiers were led by their senior NCO, Regimental Sergeant Major (RSM) Turner of the Royal Warwickshire Regiment. Mistaking Dixie for an airman of inferior rank, he proceeded to tear him off a strip for being poorly turned out and failing to respect his superior. Dixie about turned, seized the first warrant officer's jacket he could find, returned to the hut and put Turner straight! Happily there were no other such 'misunderstandings' and the two men and the two services rubbed along together comfortably enough for the duration of their stay, which fortunately wasn't long, for six weeks later the men were again on the move and on a train heading further west away from the Russians.

The journey was another that was long and unpleasant, made worse by a shortage of food. The flow of Red Cross parcels had been severely hampered in recent months by the advances on both fronts and round the clock bombing and this noticeably began to impact on both the mood – and the health – of the prisoners, many of whom fell sick. They arrived, after a trip of some 650 kilometres, at their new 'home' of Fallingbostel on August 10. Stalag 357 (the Germans had carried the number over from Thorn) was situated on a hill near the small village of Oerbke, in flat wooded heathland that had once been a military training ground. It was now under the command of Oberst Ostmann:

On the move. Stalag Luft VI – Heydekrug.

> "Fallingbostel was not far from the concentration camp at Bergen-Belsen and it was not unusual to wake up in the morning and see a cloud of smoke hanging over our camp smelling of death. All of the Poles working outside were thin and ragged, and we guessed they were not long for the gas chambers."

The NCOs were dismayed by what they found. Although used to deprivation, Fallingbostel was in a poor state of repair: the huts were dilapidated, roofs leaked and there was little in the way of heating. Notwithstanding their discomfort, Dixie immediately set about establishing the camp administration, with Alfie once again the appointed Red Cross representative.

The morale barometer, which had held reasonably high throughout the summer months following the invasion, began to dip. Progress from the invasion beaches appeared desperately slow, and then came news of the 'defeat' at Arnhem through the Canary.

Fallingbostel was close to the major port of Bremen, bringing the prisoners closer than perhaps they might have wanted to the bombing war. By night they could watch the firework displays as target indicators fell in either actual or 'spoof' raids by the RAF, and then the glow of the fires from the docks or the neighbouring towns. By day they could glance up into the skies and see the vapour trails of hundreds of American Flying Fortresses and Liberators fulfilling their side of the continuous bombing strategy.

Christmas came and went, a miserable affair with little to cheer, save for the hope that it would be Alfie's last as a prisoner of war. More prisoners were arriving by the day, and the cramped conditions of the camp became almost unbearable. Tents had to be pitched on the open ground, and prisoners were obliged to sleep out in the cold. A rumour began to circulate that German prisoners far afield were being mistreated, and this prompted a series of reprisals: blankets, palliasses and stools were removed so that the prisoners had nothing to sit on and little to sleep with. A visiting inspector from the Protecting Power described Fallingbostel simply as 'a very bad camp'.

Escape was now far from prisoners' minds. There was neither the need, the inclination nor the energy to contemplate a home run. Orders from London were also loud and clear that it was safer to stay put. Red Cross parcels were all but non-existent, and Alfie almost redundant. His task became increasingly difficult, convincing those around him who knew nothing of the system or the process that there was no secret store and that he wasn't hiding a few extra parcels under his bed! Prisoners began stealing from one another, leading to shocking examples of violence should the culprit be caught. Such was the level of malnutrition and illness that some men died despite the very best efforts of the medical staff. A dangerous lethargy began to permeate through the camp that threatened to drag once strong men down into its depression.

The end of the war was clearly only a matter of weeks away. The prisoners knew it even if the more ardent German guards failed to accept it, though most by now were prepared to bow to the inevitable. The Ardennes offensive, which promised so much, had been little more than a propaganda show that wasted what few troops, armour and aircraft the military had been able to husband, and could have been deployed to greater effect elsewhere.

There were rumours that the prisoners might be held as hostages or even massacred at the eleventh hour. Fortunately there was no proof to either suggestion, and in early March, Dixie began organising for evacuation. Alfie, who had maintained a regular correspondence with the Red Cross, wrote to them again to ask them to husband a three-month store of supplies lest they should be over-run by the Russians and out of contact with their own armed forces:

> "The International Red Cross told us that they had managed to stack up supplies at a warehouse in Lübeck. We approached the camp commandant and explained the position. At the time, the

camp inmates were aware that they could be sent out on a long march, so Dixie persuaded the commandant to allow him and me to go to Lübeck to try and obtain some parcels and arrange for a supply to reach the camp or, if the prisoners were on the march, then the supplies could reach the columns.

Alfie and Dixie were given permission and, with an interpreter, were sent out with a five-ton truck. Again, Alfie's own words describe the journey:

"We went through the outskirts of Hamburg and saw the total devastation caused by the bombing raids. The stench of rotting flesh filled the air as no attempt had been made to clear the rubble and the dead. We were told there were as many as 50,000 dead bodies that nobody could reach. And so to Lübeck where we first had a meeting with the harbour master about supplies being bought up the canal by barge. He was quite co-operative after showing him a large jar of coffee that had been brought along on the journey for just such a purpose. We stayed overnight in a services hostel surrounded by German service men some of whom were wounded and moaned all night long. We were glad to see the dawn of the next morning so we could load our wagon and proceed back to the camp with promises that lorries would be available on the march if not before."

Alfie's brief description does not entirely do justice to what he achieved in those vital few days, nor the impact it would have in helping sustain fellow prisoners at one of the most dangerous moments of their lives. Alfie had learned that the Red Cross had established a large depot at Lübeck to provide food for the camps in northern Germany, but that the lorries required to deliver that food were simply not available. Dixie therefore requested that he and Alfie would go themselves to Lübeck, and see what could be done. The commandant, remarkably perhaps, agreed and provided a van, a Russian driver and four of his men to accompany them. Alfie, as ever, made sure that he had sufficient supplies of 'sweeteners' in the form of coffee, cigarettes and chocolate should they be needed.

At Lübeck they met with the Red Cross representative, a Swede, to ensure the contents of the parcels had not in any way been compromised. This, they were assured, was not the problem; the problem was that the parcels were in the hands of a German shipping agent, and the agent had no means of transport. They were directed to the local transport officer who declined to help. It was not practical, he said, neither was he especially inclined to assist. With the officer suddenly confronted with a tin of coffee and a few other delicacies that he had not seen since the start of the war, he became most co-operative. Arrangements were made to transport several truckloads of parcels by rail and by canal, in addition to 200 parcels that were immediately loaded into their van. Alfie was the hero of the day when some 6,000 parcels arrived at Fallingbostel – enough for half a parcel per man – on March 30, 1945.

It was Good Friday.

The day arrived when the prisoners were ordered to leave the camp. The Rhine had been crossed and the Allied ground forces could be with them within days. Staying put was safer, waiting to be overrun, but the commandant had his orders and was insistent. The men would march. It was a huge disappointment.

Dixie had already divided the men into columns of approximately 1,500-2,000 men per column. Each had with them only what they could carry, remembering that the climate in northern Germany could be especially harsh, and cold, even in spring. There was an aimlessness to their journey as the first of the columns, which included Alfie, moved out heading in a vague north-easterly direction across the vast expanse of Lüneburg Heath. Not even the guards seemed to have any idea of their final destination, nor did they seem to care. The men trudged wearily for many hours, making little headway, some pulling behind them home-made carts.

Dixie kept order, discipline and morale by cycling between the columns on a clapped-out bicycle, finding himself referred to as 'the galloping major'. Everywhere there were sounds of battle, and often the columns would find themselves mingling with streams of refugees – nearly all women and children – fleeing from their homes. Anywhere away from the battle area was safe.

Alfie's party of prisoners reached the Elbe and took the opportunity of having a wash – their first in some time. Then came news that a barge full of Red Cross parcels was awaiting them at Bleckede, but that it seemed to have been commandeered by the French. Alfie was quick to react. Although the French were insistent that the parcels belonged to them, Alfie was equally insistent that they did not, and that they belonged to the British prisoners of Stalag 357. He reinforced his insistence with a simple message that if the French did not unload the barge at once, his men would sink it. They received the parcels without further ado, the barge being unloaded in double-quick time.

The happiness of the prisoners reaching the Elbe that day contrasted with the disaster that was to befall Alfie's column on April 19. Moving large bodies of men in daylight was not without its perils. On the ground, a column of prisoners might more easily be distinguished from a body of well-armed enemy troops. But from the sky, such a distinction was not so easy to make.

The column had stopped at Gresse to the north east of Lauenburg. Alfie had arranged a store of Red Cross parcels to be kept at the local school. After overseeing their distribution, he set off along a narrow country road with a ditch on either side, and sat down to take on board a few of the delights that the packages had to offer. They could hear and then see the droning of an aircraft – several in fact – circling above them, but paid little attention. Every aircraft in the skies at that time was an Allied aircraft – the Luftwaffe had effectively been annihilated – and so there was nothing to fear. These were rocket-firing Typhoons, the RAF's latest 'tank buster' that had wreaked such terrible destruction on the German armour retreating at Falaise, not long after the invasion. Then the note in the engine began to change and the more observant could see the lead aircraft wing over into a dive. Suddenly there was panic. The unthinkable was about to happen. Somebody shouted an order to take cover but the men were too slow – and perhaps too disbelieving – to react. The voices were drowned out almost immediately with the sound of explosions as the first rockets and cannon shells thumped into the ground and into human bodies.

Some men stood up and waved frantically, desperate for the Typhoon pilots to recognise their true identity. One stood in the middle of the road with a white sheet, but was obliterated by the next rocket salvo. Only when the last of the Typhoons was coming in to attack did the penny finally drop. The pilot veered away without firing a shot, someone at last recognising the full horror of what had just happened. All around on the road, in the ditches and in the neighbouring fields there were dead and wounded, some with horrific injuries. By the end of the attack, twenty-two airmen lay dead, every one a tragedy. Probably the most tragic, however, was the death of thirty-year-old Warrant Officer William Watson who had been a prisoner for almost five years. More than fifty men were killed or wounded including at least twelve soldiers and six German guards. Many of those killed were Alfie's friends.

British and Allied forces were now no more than a dozen or so miles away from the columns of Kriegies. It was critical that lines of communication were established as soon as possible to avoid further bloodshed, mistaken or otherwise. Dixie sought permission from the German commandant to head for Lauenburg. Ostmann deliberated for some time. On the one hand his orders were to keep the columns heading north and not to surrender; on the other he wanted to avoid unnecessary loss of life or the risk of being taken by the Russians. In the event he relented and permission was granted.

What happened to Alfie over those next few days is difficult to relate in any detail. The columns of marching men were becoming increasingly fragmented and communications almost impossible. Food was a constant issue: prior to setting out the men had been given a small amount of bread and sausage, but by now their rations had run out. Cigarettes, once again, became the currency of the day, prisoners exchanging large quantities with German civilians in return for an egg or a loaf as they passed through rural villages and hamlets that until then had largely been untouched by war. Some villagers were openly hostile, spitting and throwing stones; others viewed the prisoners as a fascination, something from another world.

Prisoners who had nothing left to barter scrounged for food. Dead horses were immediately seized upon and butchered, even those whose sell-by date had long since expired. Alfie did what he could to maintain some semblance of cohesion among the men, but organising for Red Cross parcels to be in the right place at the right time in advance of their progress was proving a challenge, especially with the roads blocked by retreating armies, exhausted Kriegies and disconsolate refugees in headlong retreat.

The column with which he was marching reached Rögnitz, a small farming community of less than 200 people, on April 27. As the appointed Man of Confidence, he sought permission from the column leader, Hauptmann Seelemayer, for safe passage to move along the roads without fear of being stopped. Seelemeyer duly obliged, providing Alfie with an '*Ausweis*' (pass), written in pencil on a scrap of notepaper. He also insisted that Alfie used Dixie's bike. Loosely translated the *Ausweis* read:

April 27

Stalag 357
Rögnitz, 27.4.45
Marschstaffel
Hauptmann Seelemeyer

PASS

Warrant Officer Fripp (No 5752), prisoner of Stalag 357, is authorised as the Man of Confidence in the camp to be the go-between between Hauptmann Rieve's 'Marschgruppe' and Hauptmann Seelemeyer's. Furthermore, he is authorised to pass between Krembz and Rögnitz without interference from guards.

No Stamp.

Seelemayer
Hauptmann and Staffelführer

Liberation came in many different ways. Some of the prisoners decided to ignore orders from London and slipped away from the columns while the Germans weren't looking. Such actions still had their risks: units of the fanatical SS were still inclined to kill without thinking or remorse, including murdering their own men if needed. Escaping prisoners were therefore fair game, especially since on April 30, the Führer had committed suicide. Some groups of men continued marching until they met reconnaissance units of the advancing army. Others commandeered vehicles, preferring the direct approach.

Alfie and his cohort had found refuge in the grounds of a local *Schloss* when the British 2nd Army caught up with them and the moment of liberation arrived:

> "After three weeks of marching our headquarters staff comprising
> Dixie, myself, Cyril Aynsley, Ron Mogg and a handful of others were

at a castle, or rather sleeping in the stables. The next morning I set off on my bicycle to make contact with one of the columns and was not more than 200 yards up the road when I came across a tank, and a soldier smoothing his machine gun. I started shouting '*Kamerad! Kamerad! Luftwaffe. Air Force*' whatever I could to make sure he wouldn't shoot. He asked who I was and I told him about the castle and where our columns were situated. Within a very short space of time the tanks had reached the castle and the Germans were ousted. That night we slept in the castle and the castle's occupants slept in the stables!"

Alfie's captivity – and Alfie's war – was at last over. Two days later, the German army formally surrendered.

———————————

Alfie was at first corralled with hundreds of other former prisoners of war in a holding camp and then flown to Brussels. He eventually returned to the UK by air two days later, one of more than 300,000 prisoners of war transported by the RAF (and USAAF) as part of Operation Exodus, and was a little surprised to have to share his flight – and some of his food – with a party of Germans who were being taken for interrogation. He finally arrived at 106 Personnel Reception Centre (PRC) RAF Cosford on May 9, 1945, having missed the VE-Day celebrations, a matter that irked him at the time and in later years. At Cosford he was duly processed. This process included a medical examination, and the five-and-a-half years Alfie had spent as a prisoner had taken its toll, but not his sense of humour:

"One of the tests that they gave us was the 'whisper' test to see how our hearing had been affected. They did this to one of the men and to the whisper 'whisky' he replied 'yes I don't mind if I do'. They decided there was nothing wrong with his hearing or his state of mind."

Alfie was suffering from severe malnutrition and his stomach had shrunk. His first meal comprised a crab salad which although delicious, his stomach almost immediately rejected. His body was deloused so many times that he felt he was permanently covered in white powder. Eventually, after a period of four weeks of recovery and rebuilding his strength, the authorities were happy to dispatch Alfie on immediate indefinite leave, and so he started out for Wimborne where his family was waiting:

> "When I got to Southampton there was an announcement for me to
> get off the train. I did as I was told and there was Vera."

It was a tearful yet happy reunion, and Vera was appalled at how Alfie looked. The
last few months of the war had probably been the worst, and Alfie's weight had
plummeted to a little over six stone. With his head shaven because it had been
infested with lice, he looked for all-the-world to Vera like a hardened convict, rather
than the brave and handsome husband who had left England a lifetime ago. The pair
then boarded the train and continued the journey home.

Peace could begin at last.

Alfie and fellow Kriegies looking happy and relaxed after their release.

————EPILOGUE————

Alfie's period of incarceration eclipsed virtually every one of his contemporaries, having been kept in no fewer than twelve camps between being shot down on October 16, 1939 and finally liberated on May 6, 1945.

For a brief period, Alfie enjoyed some small element of celebrity, even being asked for tea with the Countess of Shaftesbury – his erstwhile benefactor. He was able to tell her how vital her parcels, and her support, had been during his imprisonment. Her son had also been a POW in Italy and he and Alfie shared their experiences.

Five-and-a-half years away meant a period of re-adjustment and re-acclimatisation:

> "You could sit in an armchair and people would be talking to you but you heard nothing. You were just pleased because you were sitting in a comfortable armchair. When you went out, you were convinced that everyone was staring at you.
>
> "We were debriefed at Cosford: they made us familiar with what had happened during the war – rations, clothing, how people had taken the Blitz etc – and how that had affected people mentally. This was a way of bringing us back to normal. There was certainly no recognition of anything like post-traumatic stress or anything like that."

It was by no means the end of Alfie's Royal Air Force career. After a month's leave, he was posted to Berwick-upon-Tweed at the opposite end of the country, with no hope of getting home at the weekend or on leave. It was an ill reward for such a long absence from his wife. He was not impressed and said so to the Countess, explaining his position. Her influence was such that within a month he was posted to RAF Tarrant Rushton in Dorset. There for around six months, he was ordered to take a refresher course in navigation (and especially astro navigation) to resume his flying career, and posted to Bishopscourt in Ireland.

Having signed on for twenty-four years service, they determined Alfie was in fact too old for flying and was told he would have to revert to his 'basic' trade as an electrical and wireless mechanic, but with a twist. Alfie was commissioned, and attended a six-month radar course at Cranwell. He passed out as a pilot officer, Alfie remembering that his father was less impressed with his son being an officer than him being selected to play hockey for the RAF!

In 1948, Alfie was posted to 5 AHQ, RAF Habbaniya in Iraq but returned within a year to take an appointment as signals officer at RAF Calshot. He was promoted flying officer and spent time preparing the mighty Sunderland flying boats for their move to Pembroke Dock and thence onward to Hamburg where the RAF was establishing a servicing station in support of the Berlin Airlift. The Sunderlands would fly in supplies using the great lake at Wannsee, and Alfie would recall the not unusual sight of a dead German or Russian soldier floating by, a grim reminder of the bitter conflict that had raged five years before and was even now at last surrendering its dead.

> "It was ironic that they had starved me for five-and-a-half years and yet here I was now risking my life to feed them. We had to fly in using a defined corridor and if you strayed out of that corridor you could end up in trouble."

Alfie took a code and cypher course and was commended by Coastal Command for his assiduousness in teaching others the art. In 1954 he returned to his old stomping ground of Iraq (1 AHQ, RAF Habbaniya), this time taking his family with him:

> "Life was very hectic. There were twelve messes, and Christmas would start in early December and end in January! There were huge Olympic-sized pools for officers and men and we had a bungalow near the officers' club and would often visit the casino at night, leaving the children sleeping in the open with just a mosquito net upon them.
>
> "Our daily routine comprised making sure that communications

between Bahrain, Vasda, Oman etc and all of the consulates were maintained. I would connect not just the consulates but also the oil fields and RAF Regiments and RAF stations to make sure that if there were any danger, they could contact us. I would also fly around in an Avro Anson taking code books to the stations once a month in case the codes were broken.

"During the summer months it got very hot, and we would send the troops to the hills north of Iraq. One of the WAAFs fell off a donkey and we thought she had broken her neck. She hadn't but she was badly injured and we had to fly up there and airlift her back. The runway was just a dusty path about 200 yards long. Landing was extremely difficult but taking off was even worse, especially with the extra load."

On his return to the UK eighteen months later he was posted to RAF Beachy Head in charge of Radar Type 80, on one occasion tracking the aircraft of the Russian premier on his visit to the UK. Further postings followed to Andover (HQ Maintenance Command) and to the Electrical Engineering sections at RAF Gibraltar, Uxbridge and HQ Support Command.

While in Gibraltar he was made captain of the inter-service hockey team (having already represented the RAF at Yatesbury) and broke his nose in the final (Alfie played hockey until he was sixty). In Gibraltar he was responsible for all of the wireless and radar installations on 'The Rock', and would often accompany visiting dignitaries to keep them on the right side of the track.

Alfie retired from the RAF in June 1969 (he was fifty-five) in the rank of squadron leader. He may have made a higher rank, but believes his focus on sport was to prove his undoing, a fact he never regretted. He took a year out to renovate his home in Bournemouth with his wife and afterwards pursued a career in education, finally retiring after a spell teaching at Brockenhurst College.

Alfie talked little to his family about his war experiences, preferring to keep some of the darker and more difficult moments of his captivity to himself, not even sharing them with fellow Kriegies. In later life, however, his feelings changed and he was an active participant in a number of films and documentaries, especially those that sought to uncover the truth about the Great Escape – an escape that held so many painful memories. His own view of the 1963 film was typically forthright: although the first half of the film was a true and accurate depiction of Kriegie life, the second half – and most notably the motorcycle escapades of Steve McQueen – was a travesty, and insulting to the memory of those who were murdered.

In 2009 he and a number of other former POWs returned to Stalag Luft III to mark the anniversary of the Great Escape. "The most important thing is saying goodbye to those who died," he said at the scene. "The huts have all gone, but the ghosts of all those boys are here. I'm glad I came to remember Mike – you reflect back on all the memories and the people you knew. As for the Germans, I've forgiven them, but not forgotten."

He went back again in August 2011 along with a group of engineers, archaeologists and serving RAF officers to excavate for the first time ever the remains of 'Harry', the tunnel finally chosen for the Great Escape, and 'George' a sister tunnel that was never used in anger. At first, the team failed to find any remains of Harry, and in fact began digging in the wrong place. Only in the last place they looked did they finally find the tell-tale signs of a tunnel entrance, an almost perfect dark square of earth on an otherwise sandy soil canvass. Further excavations around the theatre revealed such treasures as the wheels and axel from one of the tunnel trolleys, used to haul the prisoners along the tunnel length, a radio, and various other artefacts that helped to bring the history of the camp alive. Alfie spent some considerable time on-site, pausing for a moment by the entrance to Harry to reflect on the sacrifice of the fifty and to offer up a silent prayer. He believed he could hear their souls calling to him.

———————

At his funeral at the Breakspear Crematorium on January 25, 2013, words of remembrance were spoken by the family, and by historian Dr Howard Tuck who had been with Alfie on many of his trips to Sagan. In particular, the last few lines of Aidan Crawley's 1956 masterpiece *Escape from Germany* were quoted as a fitting epitaph to a gallant airman:

> 'So ended captivity. There can be few who would choose to live through it again, but there must be many who still draw inspiration from the knowledge that much can be endured and to those who have once lost it, freedom is worth all the sacrifices which have been made for it.'

Appendix 1

MIKE CASEY ——— AND THE ——— GREAT ESCAPE

When Mike Casey was shot down, for the first few days and weeks in captivity he remained close to his men. But as an officer, it was inevitable that he would soon be separated, and Alfie would not hear of his pilot again until the dreadful news that Mike had been shot whilst attempting to escape in 1944.

The story of Mike Casey is worth a book in its own right, and one day perhaps somebody will afford his memory that honour. His bravery, both as an airman and an escapee, cannot be in any doubt.

First and foremost, Mike was a tunnel man, preferring to escape under rather than over the wire. His first tunnel was at the Air Force Transit Camp (Dulag Luft), where he found himself, in the summer of 1940, as part of the permanent staff under his former OC, Wing Commander Day. A tunnel was started under the floor of the senior French officer's living room, but the conditions were far from ideal. The tunnel continually flooded, and a decision was reluctantly taken to stop digging. The tunnel was re-opened in the early spring of 1941 and the flood water drained away. Digging in earnest carried on through April and May until the excavations were completed and the date fixed for departure, Whitsun Sunday.

Some eighteen prisoners were picked for the breakout, including Squadron Leader

Roger Bushell who would later find fame as 'Big X' – the head of the officers' escape committee. In the event, Bushell opted not to escape from the tunnel, but made a break that same night from a shed on the sports field and got as far as the Swiss border before being recaptured literally yards from freedom. Mike and his fellow tunnelers all made it safely out of the camp, but all were equally quickly rounded up. Mike was in fact one of the last of the seventeen to make the break, and with his escape partner headed south. The pair walked for twenty-four hours, trying to put as much distance as they could between themselves and the camp. They sheltered in a wood overnight before setting off early the following morning for another day of hard slog. Approaching a small village near Darmstadt, they were unlucky to be seen and stopped by a local policeman. Mike tried to bluff his way out but the policeman wasn't easily fooled and immediately demanded to see their papers. The game was up. Mike was not able to show any documentation and was immediately arrested and thrown into the local gaol. They were thence taken by bus to a civilian prison in Frankfurt and then to Barth.

Mike was one of those purged from Barth in the spring of 1942 and transported to the 'escape-proof' Stalag Luft III at Sagan. Almost immediately, under the auspices of the 'X' organisation, the prisoners began to dig, starting no fewer than three tunnels, all of which were quickly discovered or had to be abandoned. For a period of time, Mike volunteered to be one of a handful of 'ghosts' – prisoners who 'disappeared' from the sight of the Germans to give the impression that they had escaped, or to confuse their guards during *Appel*. It was widely recognised that the longer an escape could go undetected, the better the chances for those who were free beyond the wire. Mike continued this farcical game of cat and mouse with his hosts for almost six weeks before he was eventually uncovered and the Germans realised they had been duped. He paid for his misdemeanour with a spell in the Cooler.

So much has been written about the details of the Great Escape, and the three tunnels 'Tom', 'Dick' and 'Harry' that they do not need to be repeated here. Mike's initial role was as a '*Trap Führer*', protecting the entrance to 'Tom'. By sheer bad luck the trap was discovered and the prisoners concentrated their efforts on Harry. Mike was given overall responsibility for trap security, as well as creating and securing a number of 'hides' to conceal forged papers, compasses, maps, clothing and other essential escape equipment.

When the night of the break arrived and dusk fell, Mike Casey said his farewells to his fellow prisoners in hut 122 with a cheery wave and joking with them that the time had come again for another 'run in the woods'. He reported to the hut controller and Mike walked calmly out of the door and entered hut 109 by the south door. He went directly to his allocated room and again reported to the controller. With a check on the time sheet and yet another farewell, Mike made his way up the corridor of hut 109 and when it was safe, the far door was opened and he ran beside the firepool until he reached the steps of hut 104. The door opened as if on cue and Mike was met by fellow Kriegie Dave Torrens who gave him a room and a bunk. The organisation that night was second to none, and a world away from the somewhat haphazard and positively amateur attempts of the early years. Every thirty seconds the door of the hut would open again to let another would-be escaper pass, until the room was bulging with men and their escape paraphernalia, waiting anxiously for the time to go.

At the allotted hour, one by one the prisoners moved along the hut until it was their turn to enter the tunnel. The first men to make the break had discovered that the tunnel had finished short of the trees, and the exit was in open ground between the woods and the perimeter fence. A warning signal had been hastily agreed and for some period of time this worked effectively. A length of rope ran from the mouth of the tunnel to the trees, and a controller tugged on the rope to show that the passage was clear and it was safe to come out. Progress was steady if somewhat slow; the sheer volume of prisoners in the confines of such a narrow passage had caused some damage to the tunnel, making it even more difficult to transport the escapers from one end to the other along the makeshift trolley track. The difficulty was further compounded when the lights went out as a result of an air raid, although this ultimately worked in the prisoners' favour. What was clear to everyone as the night progressed was that the ambitious target of freeing 250 prisoners in one go was unlikely to be reached, and as the total passed eighty of men already clear of the camp or in the process of escape, the organisers agreed to call a halt – just as the first sounds of rifle fire were heard. But by then, Mike was already running full tilt through the woods.

Mike remained on the run for several days before being caught, and on March 28 he was taken to Görlitz prison to be reunited with a number of his fellow escapers. Then the questioning began, followed by the threats of execution. Mike was told he would be sent to the guillotine, a favoured method of execution by the Gestapo. Two days later, Mike was seen with five others being led away in handcuffs. They were never seen again.

Officially, Mike Casey's death is recorded as having taken place on March 31, 1944 – a week after the Great Escape. He, and forty-nine others, had been executed on the direct orders of Hitler, orchestrated by Heinrich Himmler. After the war, the perpetrators of the murders were all hunted down and brought to trial. Wilhelm Scharpwinkel, the Breslau Gestapo chief, was held accountable for the deaths of all of those who had disappeared from the Görlitz gaol, although he did not pull the trigger himself. Scharpwinkel avoided the hangman – although his testimony was read out in court – and he was reported to have died in a Russian camp in 1947.

The remains of Michael James Casey are buried at the Poznan Old Garrison Cemetery in Poland.

'JOHNNIE' GREENLEAF

Squadron Leader Edward John Greenleaf DSO, DFC joined the RAF in September 1930 as a Trenchard 'Brat', passing the entrance exam (Entry 22) with ease. One of the few identified for pilot training, by the outbreak of war Johnnie was a sergeant pilot with 57 Squadron, completing a tour of operations and enjoying a well-earned rest. Commissioned in January 1942, Johnnie exchanged the twin-engined Blenheim for the much faster De Havilland Mosquito, quickly gaining a reputation as an exceptional flyer. Twice Mentioned in Despatches in early 1944, Johnnie was chosen as one of a handful of pilots from 571 and 692 Squadrons to take part in a 'Gardening' sortie in November 1944 to drop mines in the Kiel Canal – a dangerous occupation – flying at low level against a target strongly defended by flak, searchlights and balloons.

Shortly after dropping his own mine, Johnnie – by now a squadron leader – was turning away from the target when his Mosquito was hit by flak. The shell splinters killed the navigator (Pilot Officer Ken Rendell – described by one contemporary as 'the life and soul of the crew room') and seriously injured Johnnie in the face and arm. Despite intense pain and fatigue, he made it home to an emergency landing at Woodbridge and received an immediate DSO for his actions. He later added the Distinguished Flying Cross before once again becoming tour expired and being appointed to serve on the staff of the AOC 8 Group, Air Commodore Donald Bennett.

Johnnie retired from the RAF in 1958, retaining the rank of squadron leader. He died in September 2010 at the age of ninety-five.

W G 'ABIE' ABRAMS

William George Abrams was originally from Portsmouth and joined the RAF soon after the end of the First World War. For almost all of his service career he was involved with flying boats in overseas squadrons. He began flying with 201 (FB) Squadron in the early 1920s and in July 1930 was posted to the Home Aircraft Depot at RAF Henlow. By 1936 he was with 205 Squadron as a flight lieutenant, and one of the squadron's most experienced pilots entrusted with flying some of the most challenging routes, often with senior officers as passengers. Not long after the outbreak of the Second World War he found himself back with 201 Squadron, but this time as its officer commanding, a position he held between April and December 1941. One of his last appointments was as station commander of RAF Felixstowe (1945-46). He retired from the RAF as a group captain.

JAMES 'DIXIE' DEANS

James 'Dixie' Deans was a Glaswegian who was educated at North Kelvinside Secondary School before joining the RAF in 1936. Flying with 77 Squadron on the outbreak of war, he was said to have been on his twenty-fifth operation when his aircraft was shot down over Holland in September 1940. His exploits within the prison camps are legendary, and when he was finally released the award of an MBE for his efforts was considered insufficient recognition by a good many of his fellow Kriegies. After the war, Dixie became a senior administrative officer at the London School of Economics before retiring due to ill health. He suffered for most of his adult life from multiple sclerosis, but that did not prevent him from becoming president of the RAF ex-POW Association and working tirelessly for their cause. He died in 1989.

CYRIL AYNSLEY

The son of a Penrith grocer, Cyril Aynsley was a journalist before the war having cut his teeth on the *Carlisle Journal* before moving on to the *Daily Mirror* and then ultimately the *Daily Express*. He enlisted in the RAF in 1940 and trained as a wireless operator. Posted to 15 Squadron he was flying in the crew of Flight Lieutenant R P Wallace-Terry on the night of September 7, 1941 when their Short Stirling was hit by flak during an attack on Berlin and crashed. Happily, every member of the crew made it out in one piece, and Cyril was sent to Stalag Luft III. After the war, he returned to the *Express*, and was appointed OBE in 1974.

PETER THOMAS

Peter Thomas was the son of a solicitor at Llanrwst. After Epworth College he went up to Jesus College Oxford to read law but interrupted his studies to join the RAF. Having qualified as a sergeant pilot he was flying as the second pilot with 51 Squadron on the night of June 19 1941 when his aircraft (a Whitley V) failed to return from an attack on Düsseldorf. During his four years in captivity he continued his legal studies, representing a number of prisoners including one who had been accused of sabotage. Called to the Bar in 1947 he took silk in 1965, and in the interim was selected as the Conservative MP for Conway. Thomas had a long and distinguished career in politics, becoming the first ever Conservative secretary of state for Wales and the first Welsh chairman of the Conservative party. He retired in 1987 and was created a life peer.

Appendix 2

LETTER TO
—THE BRITISH RED CROSS—
SOCIETY

To: The British Red Cross Society
St James's Place
London SW1

Date: 23rd August 1943

Dear Sir

Before submitting the following report I would like to convey the gratitude and appreciation of all the prisoners in this camp for the efficient way in which you and your staff have maintained the vital parcel service which is so essential to our well-being here.

In my letter dated 1st August 1943 addressed to the International Red Cross, Geneva, I mentioned the consignment of British Red Cross Parcels which arrived here, but in the event of this extract not reaching you, I will repeat it here:

Extract from above letter:

"The bulk of this consignment appears to be rather old stock, and although the contents are intact they are in somewhat dilapidated condition. However they have been very well received here as we have been living on Canadian Red Cross food parcels since our arrival and a more varied diet can now be obtained.

"I wish to report that two brands of meat contained in these parcels viz Harris Meat Roll and Tyne Products Ltd Corned Beef Hash are in a bad condition and a large percentage inedible. I understand that a complaint was sent from Stalag Luft III concerning Harris Meat Roll.

"Owing to the non-existence of cooking facilities in the barrack rooms in this camp we have been forced to adopt a system of communal messing whereby all food is prepared by the cookhouse. This leads to a number of complications in distribution and at present these could be overcome by consignments of bulk food as opposed to parcels. We fully realise that it may not be convenient or possible at all times to send bulk food so I leave the matter entirely in your hands."

Our present stock of parcels, at the standard issue of one parcel per week, will last until 31.08.43. A telegram has been despatched to Geneva advising them of this fact, together with information that we now have available storage space for 30,000 parcels. We feel that it would be advantageous in having this reserve as the camp strength will be increasing rapidly to 6,000 men.

The contents of the BRC food parcels are wholesome, nourishing and of very high food standard. I am sure that all your staff who spend much time and energy in research, packing etc are compensated for their efforts by the knowledge of the healthy and well-nourished state of the prisoners of war at this camp. To these people we extend our sincere thinks, not belittling however the splendid work carried out by other departments. The only suggestion I have to offer is that if possible, wood wool, as used in the packing of the Scottish food parcels, be substituted for the present paper packing or, if this is impractical, that the chocolate be protected by a stiff cardboard wrapping.

Next of Kin Parcels

The consignments of the next of kin parcels arriving now are dated April and May although there are many January parcels still outstanding. Have you received notification of shipments being lost during the period of January and February? Different packing centres still appear to vary considerably in the matter of forbidden articles and it is requested that a standard list be sent to centres in order to clarify the position. It would also be of great help if you could forward a list to this camp. The packaging of parcels is very good indeed. The following articles are being confiscated from parcels in this camp: yellow polishing dusters; navy blue shorts; indelible pencils.

The number of next of kin parcels received from 28.6.43 to 19.8.42 was 1,094.

For the information of the prisoners here it would be of great interest if you would kindly outline the principles of the coupon system with regard the next of kin parcels. We have received no official information about this and the references from private letters are apt to be somewhat misleading.

Blankets and pyjamas are not now sent out by you in the bulk consignments of clothing for POWs and it is therefore impossible to equip new prisoners with these items. Would it be possible for you to notify the next of kin of new prisoners to include these articles in the *first* clothing parcel that they dispatch?

Private Cigarette Parcels

Generally speaking, these parcels are now arriving fairly regularly and except for a few cases [are arriving] in good condition. However, most of the parcels sent by the Anglo-American Tobacco Co contain no receipt card and the recipient of the parcel is often unaware of the identity of the sender. To obviate this would it be possible for you to approach the above company and request them either to include a card giving the name of the donor and the date the parcel was sent or to print these particulars on the outer address label?

The number of cigarette parcels received from 28.6.43 to 18.8.43 was 4,245.

Book Parcels

A similar system to the one mentioned in the previous paragraph would improve the present arrangements regarding books that are sent by the booksellers ie the inclusion of a receipt card with the date of dispatch, donor's name, recipient, and number of books. This scheme has been adopted by the New Bodleian Library through the booksellers, D H Blackwell Ltd.

General

With regard to sports equipment and musical instruments, would it be possible to supply us with the details concerning the shipment of these? At present it is known that these items may be sent to you for dispatching here and several cases have been received together with the receipt cards. The normal time of transit is in the region of eight to ten months.

The medical parcels which are sent by air mail are arriving regularly, the time taken for delivery being about one month.

The cardboard packing of gramophone records is very unsatisfactory and a large percentage of the records packed this way have arrived broken. The Decca Gramophone Co dispatch their records in wooden containers and it has been ascertained that these records have, except in very rare incidences, arrived intact. Could you therefore communicate this fact to the other gramophone companies?

In closing I would again like to stress how much we appreciate the wonderful work you are doing for us. Will you please convey out heartfelt thanks to your patient and hardworking staff.

Yours very sincerely

A G Fripp

cc James A G Deans. Camp Leader

Appendix 3

LETTER TO THE
—RED CROSS AND ST JOHN—
WAR ORGANISATION

To: The Red Cross and St John War Organisation
St James's Place
London SW1

Date: 7th January 1944

Dear Sir,

I am forwarding together with this letter the following returns: Returns of invalid comforts and medical parcels; statement of communal parcels for the period 5th June-31st December; statement of private parcels for the period 5th June-31st December. Copies of the above returns have been forwarded under separate cover to the International Red Cross, Geneva.

Our camp strength now stands at 3,100 but a new compound here will be opening in about a month's time capable of holding another 2,000 men. When this compound opens, the International Red Cross, Geneva, will be informed immediately by telegram, requesting larger reserve, so that if at a later date communications become disrupted, we shall have a reserve at hand to carry us on.

Regarding the standard food parcels that are arriving now, we are pleased to say that almost without exception the contents are in excellent condition on arrival here. Unfortunately one of the products ie the Oxton Brand tins of stew does not come up to the usual high standard. This is rather surprising because all of the Oxton Brand products in the Christmas parcels were found to be of excellent quality. The only criticism I have to offer regarding these Christmas parcels is that a certain number of the cakes were covered with mildew; this being probably due to dampness before sealing. I am sure you will be pleased to know that Christmas here went with a swing and the spirit of the prisoners was exceptionally high.

As seen from the attached statement, there was a decided falling off of incoming private parcels during December. This was due to the increased traffic during the xmas period and has been experienced in previous years. The personal clothing parcels arriving in now were mostly despatched in August last. Except for the above temporary hold up, private parcels of all types have been arriving regularly and, in most cases, in good condition.

Information regarding invalid comforts, surgical and medical parcels is being dealt with in a letter which is being sent under separate cover.

Before closing I would like, on behalf of the POWs in this camp, to thank you for your untiring efforts on our behalf. We sincerely appreciate these efforts that you have continually made for us and we know that the high standard of efficiency that you have shown in the past will continue in the future.

Yours very sincerely

A G Fripp

Appendix 4

LIST OF 57 SQUADRON —— LOSSES IN FRANCE —— 1939

OCTOBER 13

Blenheim I – L1138 – shot down

Wing Commander Harry Day	Prisoner of war
Sergeant Eric Hillier	Killed in action
AC2 Frederick Moller	Killed in action

Blenheim I – L1147 – crash landed

Pilot Officer Clive Norman	Safe
Sergeant Edwards	Safe
AC1 Terrence Jervis	Safe. Later killed 9.7.40

OCTOBER 16

Blenheim I – L1141 – shot down

Flying Officer Mike Casey	POW. Murdered 29.3.44
Sergeant Alfie Fripp	Prisoner of war
AC1 J 'Paddy' Nelson	Prisoner of war

NOVEMBER 6

Blenheim I – L1145 – shot down

Pilot Officer Alexander Morton	Killed in action
Sergeant Geoffrey Storr	Killed in action
AC1 Frederick Twinning	Killed in action

NOVEMBER 7

Blenheim I – L1325

Pilot Officer H R Bewlay	Prisoner of war
Sergeant S McIntyre	Prisoner of war
AC1 T P Adderley	Prisoner of war

NOVEMBER 15

Blenheim I – L1246 – flying accident

Sergeant Stanley Farmer	Killed
Flight Sergeant Frederick Bowden	Killed
LAC Ivor Partlow	Killed

NOVEMBER 16

Blenheim I – L1148 – force landed

Sergeant Gilmore	Interned in neutral Belgium
Sergeant Turnidge	Interned in neutral Belgium
AC1 Terrence Jervis	Interned. Later killed 9.7.40

NOVEMBER 23

Blenheim I – L1129 – flying accident

| Pilot Officer Oliver Hume | Killed |
| Two crew safe. | |

Appendix 5

OFFICERS OF
——————57 SQUADRON,——————
OCTOBER 1939

Name	Notes including fate (where known)
Wing Commander Harry Day	Shot down.
Squadron Leader Arthur Garland	Assumed command after Day shot down. Later group captain.
Flight Lieutenant S S 'Jock' Fielden	Captain RA.
Flight Lieutenant Geoffrey Wyatt	DFC. Retired as group captain.
Flight Lieutenant John Roncoroni	DFC as OC 77 Squadron as wing commander.
Flight Lieutenant James 'Freddie' Foulsham	DFC, AFC. Killed in action with 109 Squadron as a squadron leader on a 'heavy Oboe' raid on July 20, 1944.

Flying Officer Eric Nind

Awarded DFC as acting wing commander with 97 Squadron.

Flying Officer Clive Norman

Resigned commission February 13, 1942.

Flying Officer John Hird

Promoted squadron leader March 1942.

Flying Officer William Adam

Killed in flying accident March 15, 1940.

Flying Officer Mike Casey

Shot down October 16, 1939. Murdered.

Pilot Officer H G Graham Hogg

Killed in action April 14, 1940.

Pilot Officer Roi Saunders

Killed May 22, 1940.

Pilot Officer Alexander Morton

Killed November 6, 1940.

Pilot Officer John Grant

Flight Lieutenant June 1941.

Pilot Officer Archibald Stewart

DFC and DFC (US) as wing commander. Retired as air commodore having commanded 167, 322 and 122 Squadrons and led 125 Wing. Was Air Attaché in Warsaw, 1953.

Pilot Officer Francis Buckingham

Equipment officer.

Pilot Officer Harry 'Pop' Bewlay

Shot down November 7, 1939.

Pilot Officer Oliver Hume

Killed in flying accident November 23, 1939.

ACKNOWLEDGEMENTS AND SOURCES

Official Records

RAF Halton – Entry 22 examination results and archive
AIR 27/537 – Operations Record Book 57 (Bomber) Squadron
AIR 27/1177 – Operations Record Book 201 (Flying Boat) Squadron
AIR 27/1214 – Operations Record Book 205 (Flying Boat) Squadron

Personal Interviews

Alfie Fripp
Air Commodore Charles Clarke OBE
Andy Wiseman
Eric Hookings
Cal Younger

Audio/Video

The life and World War Two experiences of Alfie 'Bill' Fripp as told to Patricia and Robert Fripp
Archive interviews (1974) with Dixie Deans, Peter Thomas, Ron Mogg, Cyril Aynsley

Select Bibliography

Above the Trenches	Franks, Shores and Guest
Aircraft of the Royal Air Force	Owen Thetford.
Blenheim Boy	Richard Passmore (Roger Peacock)
Clipped Wings	Donald Blair
Escape from Germany	Aidan Crawley
Footsteps on the Sands of Time	Oliver Clutton-Brock
Moving Tent	Richard Passmore
No Flight from the Cage	Calton Younger
RAF Bomber Command Losses	William Chorley
Tedder: Quietly in Command	Vincent Orange
The Poacher's Brats	Frank Whitehouse
The Sergeant Escapers	John Dominy (Ron Mogg)
Under the Wire	William Ash
Valiant Wings	Norman Franks
'Wings' Day	Sydney Smith

Books on the Great Escape

A Gallant Company	Jonathan Vance
The Great Escape	Paul Brickhill
The Great Escape	Anton Gill
The Great Escapers	Tim Carroll
The Longest Tunnel	Alan Burgess

———PERSONAL THANKS———

My first thanks must of course go to Alfie's family who encouraged me from the outset to record Alfie's story, and continued to graciously allow me to complete *The Last of the 39-ers* after Alfie's sudden and unexpected loss. It is invidious to pick out individuals, but I would especially like to thank Robert Fripp, Sue and David Dorrell and Julian Gibbs for their time, practical assistance and good humour at every stage. This project could not have been completed without them, and I hope they are happy with the result. It is a privilege to have met them.

Colin Higgs deserves special mention for having the foresight to have put many of Alfie's memories on record, and for allowing me access to his archive. With his colleague Bruce Vigar, they have recorded a great many veterans' experiences and hope over time to bring these experiences to a wider audience (www.aflyinghistory.com).

Min Larkin and Francis Hanford at The Trenchard Museum at RAF Halton once again came up with the goods, helping me find out more about Alfie's time at Halton and Cranwell, and John Francis of the Cranwell Apprentices Association was most helpful in steering me towards *The Poacher's Brats*. Bill Chorley helped once again with details around Alfie's first Blenheim crash, and Dominik Rosch provided help with translations of original German documents.

To my publisher John Davies and my editor Sophie Campbell at Grub Street I would like to extend another huge thanks, especially for their pragmatism and patience in the final stages of preparing Alfie's story, and for extending my deadline! Grub Street continues to publish the best books within this space and I am proud to have worked with them on this our fifth book together.

My work colleagues Iona McIntyre and Alex Simmons as always showed enough interest to at least be polite, and keep me relatively sane when my instincts may be leading me in another direction! And to Paul just a few words: six and five.

Last but never least, my gratitude to Elaine and the boys, Matt and James, who thanks to the wonder of exams have had other things on their minds and have left me in comparative peace!

Sean Feast

INDEX